Will the Real King Assassin Please Stand Up from Sanity to Insanity?

Will the Real King Assassin Please Stand Up from Sanity to Insanity?

KIM L. SMALLS

ARPress
ILLUMINATING IDEAS
EMPOWERING VOICES

ARPress LLC
45 Dan Road Suite 5
Canton MA 02021
Hotline: 1(888) 821-0229
Fax: 1(508) 545-7580

Ordering Information:
Quantity sales. Special discounts are available on quantity purchases by corporations, associations, and others. For details, contact the publisher at the address above.

Printed in the United States of America.

ISBN-13:   Softcover   979-8-89330-833-4
           eBook   979-8-89330-834-1

Library of Congress Control Number: 2024902566

CONTENTS

PREFACE

Kim L. Smalls was born to the late Mr. and Mrs. Robert L. Smalls as a baby boomer. She was educated by the public school system when prayer was a part of their protocol. She was baptized at the tender and impressionable age of seven.

Kim later received her Bachelor of Science degree at New York Institute of Technology in 1979 and majored in Sociology,Social Work. She was a Case Manager by profession, lived the life of parties, drugs, tobacco and alcohol which included the riotous living of men. At the age of twenty, she gave birth to her daughter, Nikeya.

Kim is loving, trustworthy, generous and kind to a fault. She is humble, meek, lowly, often misunderstood and taken advantage of by most as a prodigal child of God. She was living and learning the hard life of schizephrenia in the wilderness for over 30 years.

God is an active player and role model in Kim's life. She has been delivered, set free for now and completely sold out to Christ since 2000 the year of our Lord.

Will the real King assassin please stand up from sanity to insanity sowed while her Christian experience flourished to the height of the government, militarized Antichrist! Kim could not stand alone in the truth of her own sanity as she believed the enemy waged war. Kim's pursuit of social justice and criminal reform were pending and loomed forward in lawlessness and normlessness in redemption by the highest of God.

Domestic terrorism and her black skin mattered against the Special Forces of evil to cover up this crime by character assassination. The powers of darkness again victimized Jesus Christ and the late great Reverend

Martin Luther King Jr. as Kim watched and suffered spiritually their outrageous plan to persecute her as a witness. This is her testimony dared to be given in church and on the couch due to expletives and another new millennium.

IN THE BEGINNING

This narrative is about the extraordinary and mystifying life of a child of God. I was not the saint I was called to be at the tender age of seven. I was rebellious, stubborn, and disobedient to my mom and the Holy Spirit while growing up in Queens, New York. I hadn't learned my life's lessons until I was completely pruned at the age of fifty-seven and could favorably understand the golden years of all her corrections. My mother passed away on Labor Day, 2012.

Jesus Christ assisted to prevent negative, ungodly episodes in my life. But I never listened to my first thought, and didn't realize how much I needed Him until 1979. My life was wayward and out of control. He finished training me by using Satan (Rev. 12:9) to lead me to the straight and narrow (Matt.7:14) path of Christianity according to the King James Version of the Holy Bible (Heb.12:6).

In 1974, I graduated six months early from high school. On the first day of college was when I met the seed giver of my child. We made a commitment, but during the semester, I lost my interest. I continued to spend the night over his house in Long Island. Over the years, he became just a sexual encounter, which resulted in major heartbreak by the company that he kept. His baby mama drama became unbearable and horrifying. Her spirit, which I believed was abetted by the Feds years later, insisted upon haunting me.

It was the year of 1979 at the police academy for a New York railroad when peer pressure led to my being "forced out." A rookie cop suggested we pad the books, and I turned us in on a monitored telephone line at police headquarters. Consequently, I thought this officer became a decoy for the Ku Klux Klan in the South Bronx as confided in me by a brother from an adjoining railroad. I was an African American sister in a backslidden condition. I lied to myself about wanting to be sincere. But it was too late. I ended up in the emergency room at Elmhurst Hospital.

I saw my first vision "on the job" and yearned to become a detective. However, despite my heart's desire by the grace of God, I performed a miracle on the tracks. I was placed under scrutiny and surveillance by the Special Investigation Unit (SIU) of their Communications Department as a petty thief and a vessel used by God. The miracle confirmed and forewarned that SIU pursued to intentionally blow their cover as we approached the red light. It was just as I had suspected. I was being followed. Finally, I resigned.

On December 25.1982, I started employment at the US Postal Service at the John F. Kennedy airmail facility while visions of monumental, animated caricatures of kings invaded the site, and seeing the spirit of my deceased father led to my resignation.

It was 1983 when I believed I was being followed by the acclaimed Federal Bureau of Investigation. I thought I was under surveillance as an invasion of my privacy continued. I believed my civil rights were violated as a law-abiding citizen. I was unemployed and under the radar. Yet my black militancy had faded, and there was a holy quietness before the storm.

God allowed Reverend Dr. Martin Luther King Jr. to wake up out of his eternal sleep. The angel confronted an officer he knew whom he said had stolen money from him or a mystery of a contract (Eccles. 9:4-12). "The thief cometh not but to steal and to kill and destroy" (John 10:10).

I believed this Special Investigation Unit had taken to the skies. I lived on the sixth floor in the projects with my daughter. Jesus, in His own way, said that the visions from the Almighty God allowed my "hearsay rights as a citizen" of this country and as part of His earthly kingdom to witness the confrontation (Acts 12:7-11, Luke 24:23). He was frightened by Dr. King's appearance, and I was frightened by his appearance. I thought it was the Klan. Henceforth, the adversary proved that the fear of losing anonymity, credibility, and power were jeopardized by my God. I thought I was in the middle of a war involving Dr. King secrets, the FBI, and the King of kings. The following day, I believed they resorted to the supernatural, or the occult, to persecute and destroy me by any means necessary.

My Lord and Savior, Jesus Christ, used His omnipotence against the, in my opinion, FBI, who violated my freedom. They sought to torture me. I was accessible to them in the flesh and blood of mankind. They could no longer harass Dr. King in his angelic state (Eccles. 9:4-12). I believe the government police knowingly hid behind the guise of paranoid schizophrenia whereas time lapsed and propelled them into admitted sociopaths or the criminally insane. Disclosure of the King false profit conspiracy of silence from my visions questioned his assassination, which weighed heavily upon my back as my being diagnosed with schizophrenia.

Psychologists would say I am in denial of this serious mental abnormality because of its ramifications by society as the "insane." They cannot define that which is "normal," and so I suffer. My concerns were of psychiatrists who would overdose the illness for the sake of treatment as the solution. The visions are outside of their psychological expertise, which yielded to medicinal and therapeutic resolutions for the supernatural of spirituality. This practice threatened the altering of the belief system and the truth. I realized that deliverance by God is necessary from the occult and the imagination risks, which lead to institutionalization.

According to scripture, this was a vexation of spiritual warfare between Jesus Christ and a demonic force known as Satan, the False Prophet or the Antichrist of this world (2 Cor. 4:4). He can kill the body but not necessarily the soul (Matt.10:28). In the Word of God, Jesus promised to eradicate the works of the Devil, who discomforted me. One demonic spirit chose to linger on. But I have the faith necessary, for this too shall pass. This was His mission two thousand years ago while He walked upon the earth (1 John 3:8).

I believed the FBI created a plot to annihilate me. However, that was not in the Master's plan. I was the assaulted scapegoat between ungodly men and the spirit of Christ. The torture as an enemy of the state by sorcery, witchcraft, curses, séances, spells, incantations, voodoo—or the black arts of Africa—was merciless (Deut. 18:10-11, Acts 8:9-11). My defense came by way of the Holy Spirit, prayer, fasting, and the Word of God, or the Holy Scriptures (Matt. 17:14-21). I live today with the peace of Christ. He is a mind regulator and means life to me. When Jesus is for you, who can be against you? (Rom. 8:31).

This account bears my witness.

This indignation of theft or a mysterious contract and profanity in Reverend King's angelic state was clandestine. I wanted answers and transparency due to the misery and pain it caused by the secrecy in my life (Matt. 10:26). All sorts of questions came to mind as the men and women responded to Reverend King's demand. He exposed this criminal element by the inquiry of his money. "No weapon that is formed against me shall prosper" (Isa. 54:17).

Dr. King was livid. "Touch not mine anointed, do my prophets no harm" (Ps. 105:15). Eighteen trillion dollars in debt reflected the economic issues of this nation. There is still no debt ceiling (CNN). "For the weapons of our warfare are not carnal, but mighty through God to the pulling down of strong holds" (2 Cor. 10:4).

I became a prayer warrior in the middle of spiritual warfare. My waking moments were terrifying as a spiritual mortal of ignorance due to the inexperience of the supernatural and HooDoo. I was a powerful woman anointed by God. My faith as a believer in Christ Jesus sufficed me to survive. I perceived that their undercover operation monitored my thoughts as I searched for answers and the pursuit of a killer that was on "his job." I cited the occurrence by the heavenly host as awesome and prophetic. Jesus is the victor, and I am more than a conqueror who reigns in this war for the need to acknowledge justice. I have been redeemed.

MIRACLE ON THE TRACKS

I was a youthful, vibrant, immature, and inexperienced mother of a two-year- old, and needed a job or a career. I attended graduate school for a public administration degree conditionally at John Jay College of Criminal Justice and had just graduated with honors from New York Institute of Technology.

Two years prior to graduation, I left the rearing of a devout-Christian single-parent household to live on my own. My father died from lung cancer when I was twelve. I had just finished a course in Introduction to Public Administration and was not at all pleased with my grade. I had not taken graduate school very seriously. It was apparently not meant to be. I tried again during my mom's illness, or years later. I happened to look up as I exited class one day, and the Wanted ads caught my eye. On the billboard was a Help Wanted sign for the Railroad Police Department freight division, and I applied. I did not qualify for anything else posted. I needed the money. It wasn't until after class I was actively looking for employment. Honestly speaking, I never wanted such a dangerous position, but I took the math test anyway. I always viewed the police as a hazardous job.

I should have known what was more important. I believed this was about federal funding from the beginning and the color of my skin. Later, I found out I was not really welcome. Affirmative action in those days was prevalent, and a grade of 92 from a black female with a college degree was not a shabby test score. The Railroad was not a person-centered organization when it came down to money.

I thought something was awry when all the requirements were to take a math test. People who are naive live and learn the facts of life. However, I did think about safety first, and I knew I had a God to back me up. It was my first chance to live life on life's terms in the employment sector. I was on public assistance, had no means of support, and was poor. A background check qualified me for confirmation as a peace officer. The investigation was superficial and nothing intense. All I needed was my degree and a reference.

There were a few notable men in my life but none worthy of a serious long- lasting relationship like marriage. For the most part, their bottom line was sex, sex, and more sex.

I met Captain Junior on my very first day of full-time employment at the Railroad. His father hired me after sexually harassing me for tenure in Fort Apache, in the Bronx. I compromised myself to get ahead, so I didn't say anything. I already got the position by merit. It was my worst experience in the private sector of business and my biggest mistake of all time. Captain Junior startled me with a racist remark and requested I belittle myself as we headed back to police headquarters. He wanted me to shine the sergeant's boots. I asked myself, "Why me?" when I asked Jesus the same question. "Love your enemies" came into mind.

I thought I was compromising myself for the second time during my first employment. The Special Investigations Unit (SIU) was already following because of a telephone call to a friend. I made an admission of guilt by padding the books during the police academy. I could have sworn my allegiance to the Klan that day. It was an embarrassing and dehumanizing request in front of a white male department with whom I was struggling to build a rapport as coworker.

During the probation period by Captain Junior, I was a guilty prime candidate and a victimized target by a white accomplice of questionable integrity as a new recruit. I felt as though I was being an outcast and betrayed. I was glad Captain Senior was gone. I knew to be wary of his requests. The rookie white cop suggested padding the books. I felt guilty because I made an oath to Jesus. The rookie severed all ties with me, and I grew suspicious of him. He was quite comfortable. He felt at ease and had no problems fitting in.

The Special Investigations Unit knew about everything. The rookie cop arose through the ranks as detective while I dealt unsuccessfully with the shame and guilt of racism as a petty thief. I told the truth and covered myself by using the rookie's name. I compensated and paid it all back, which was at the most fifty dollars. I succumbed to the hatred of bigotry firsthand and eventually landed in Elmhurst Hospital Emergency Room with excruciating stomach pangs. It was never diagnosed or documented by a physician. I told no one that I was ailing. I left.

I grew up in the Christian faith and knew that God will protect me if anything serious occurred that I could not handle alone, like life-and-death situations. I unknowingly signed up with the Railroad Ku Klux Klan. Harry, a brother from the adjoining Railroad, informed me that SIU and the Railroad I belong to were Klansmen. He knew I was being followed.

In the beginning, I submitted a referral from the late reverend Dr. Timothy P. Mitchell of Ebenezer Baptist Church of Flushing, New York. I accepted the job, an act that bred the new beginnings of scandal. I was "forced out" and set up due to my own ignorance and innocence of poverty in life. Questioning SIU practices, I felt violated as well. I was waiting to be fired. The proposal by the captain painstakingly to this day had civil rights suit implications.

In the Master's plan and in His divine schedule, Jesus took on this case for the truth of my guilt-ridden status. I was not crazy. I was untrustworthy. Nevertheless, the thought of becoming a detective intrigued me until the signs of the times of my mental health, injustice, poor judgment, and self- righteousness made it no sense to stay. The Holy Spirit convinced me to leave.

My account of insufficient funds and balances of a judicial nature has been, for over the past thirty years, deemed to be bankrupt because law enforcement is unjust and corrupt. I failed and was not any better.

The secretary, who was a police officer, told me, "Just plant a knife if you have to make the story go away." The truth conflicted with lies about their course of action as being the best from the SIU as they openly followed me. They lacked fairness by threats of losing my mind.

I realize the situation could have been worse. They override daily that I resign, with blatant racism remarks and overtones. Even though normalcy as I know it had come to an end, we could no longer govern ourselves. They never asked me to leave or tell me that I was fired. They were out of my control. The inequality of racism as coworkers in a department of justice developed into harassment. I endured as lawlessness being the norm. As a social ill, racism polarized the people for whom it was established into hostile lifestyles and as murderers. It wasn't worth my sanity or even the thought of losing it.

On life's journey ensued a miracle on the tracks in the midst of enemy property in broad daylight. As SIU from the Railroad followed me, taped me, slept with me, harassed me, and frustrated the end of my employment, I was a goner. They drove me to a state of physical illness, which was never diagnosed by a medical doctor. I was diagnosed emotionally and mentally as my integrity reached an unhealthy peak.

The spiritual presence of the Holy Ghost abided and emerged on a Saturday afternoon. I laid my burdens down that Friday night. I had not prayed formally in four years. I resumed communication with Jesus Christ for the time being after much internal strife and crises with the organization. I was psychologically evaluated by a professional as "overly religious" at best and headed for a nervous breakdown, she said, if I did not resign.

What I had suspected was confirmed. My prayer consisted of confessions, repentance, suspicions of being followed, hearing voices from SIU in my environment, and feelings of being watched at a distance at night as I secured the yard. I was in imminent danger. The covert acts were blatantly executed and my sanity questioned as I prayed for confirmation, relief, a tranquil mind, comfort, and direction. I was rebellious and refused to resign. However, it was a matter of time. Spiritually, I was a mess.

The outcome of my Rorschach test was "overly religious." I saw a bear rug, Moses who could have been Jesus, Santa Claus with a tear in his eye and gifts.

The Railroad disclosed myself to me, which I finally caught on by the Spirit of the Living God. I was looking at my personality traits, and I knew I had to let go and let God. I was being forced out. I again had to deal with being a failure in life. I had not any husband, a higher education, and/or a job.

That Saturday afternoon, alongside a racist coworker, Jesus used me as His vessel. This officer eventually called me the N word. The yard was clear. There were no engines to be coupled up to the boxcars. As procedure, we checked. I touched the security lock with my right forefinger, and the boxcar derailed. He looked at me, and I looked at him. We said nothing.

SIU pulled up beside the police van and asked, "What, you want to prove how mighty you are?" They had to make a report of accountability. Approximately three weeks later, it was either my sanity or the job. I had already taken internally a lot and suffered from burnout.

I was unemployed and still feeling the aftermath of SIU. They appeared to have continued to follow by sending criminal physiological faces—misfits—in front of me as I went about my daily living in the Long Island City vicinity. I was cursed. By the depths of darkness and stillness of nights, this criminal insanity overcame me. My serious demeanor had changed into that of a fiend. For a moment or two, all I wanted to do was to kill everybody. But my God, Jesus, drained my hot blood from a murderous takeover. Finally, I believed it was a foretelling of what was yet to come, a prophecy about the Feds. I screamed as if someone was killing me, and no one in the building reported it.

I went to the Human Rights Commission to complain about the Railroad, but like in Elmhurst Hospital, the wait was totally unacceptable. The wait was unbearable in the overcrowded waiting rooms. The violations were never documented, and the excruciating stomach pains were miraculously gone. The establishment left a spiritual battle of racism, which eventually escalated into a full-fledged war between good and evil, right and wrong, God and Satan—a spiritual warfare. They left behind sacrilegious combinations of assumptions regarding my God, my power, and my life of Satanic revelations by criminal acts. I believed they confused my mind with their haunting of my lifestyle, God, my existing drug usage, and expletives of vulgar proportions. I could not believe they had lingered as a curse not in this day and age.

My presence at the Railroad was the time of the Atlanta child murders. The Railroad's violations manifested into an unholy war between the past, present, and future of my civil rights and militancy overseen by a big lie regarding a computer. I thought I had a computer for a brain as a living soul that came out of nowhere. I believed the computer used in this curse made me anxious and stifled me. The stress was unbearable. I was not a thing made by hands or a tape recorder.

I kept the aftermath of anger to myself in an unhealthy way. I could never express in ladylike terms what I thought about them. The profanity pricked my heart in the year and a half of torment, which translated later into spiritual work by Satan. This was typical of a few Railroad policemen, country Western style, subhumans in the Bronx. Their lawlessness as perpetrators committed severe fraudulent acts as models of our society. SIU violated my head by breaking into my soul, spirit, and body. However, the effectual fervent prayers of the righteous availed much (James 5:16). As a man thinks in his heart, so is he (Prov. 23:7). I knew I was not crazy. However, Jesus had already confirmed that this could lead to mental illness. I prayed for Him to explain. Although I knew nothing about mental illness, for the time being, I told Him that I was fine.

I believed the undercover of SIU followed. They lied about my ungodly lifestyle as well as my Christian beliefs of worship. I was the demon. The unthinkable was thought while horrendous acts of being a sinful, sick soul gripped my mind by thought patterns unworthy as a demon-possessed believer. I did not know I was no longer under the law of Judaism but the New Testament will and grace of Jesus Christ (Eph. 2:5). I knew him as a problem solver who died for my sins and arose on the third day with all power in heaven and earth in His hands (Matt. 28:18). Jesus did not inform me that the prayer would take over thirty years to sort out and complete from insanity to sanity.

SIU was getting careless. As I pulled out of a park, they would instantly follow. I first noticed the "tail" while in the freight yard. I could feel someone looking at me from a distance in the night while I secured the lock on the boxcar. I was written up once and had to go to a hearing when the youth from the projects broke a seal. They robbed the freight train, which was inaccessible to me. I never got a chance to check the lock that night. I explained my dilemma to the panel. Nevertheless, I was penalized approximately one hundred dollars from my pay for not prioritizing the chain of events that ensued.

I was a new driver and drove a police SUV. One day, I got caught between the tracks and an embankment. I had no sense of distance. If a detective had not come out of the office and backed the van away, I probably would have incurred serious injuries. I thought about giving up on life because the oncoming train began to hit the vehicle harder and faster. I knew I was ready to resign.

Three weeks later, I lost the credit card. I left that very same day. I planned to never look back and felt sorry to put that employment on my résumé. I definitely learned from the experience. I still had my sanity, but I was tired.

Their clandestine mission was unsuccessful due to the miracle on the tracks.

This was more than a simple case of racism, folly, and sexual harassment. They were getting sloppy and callous. Their computer was no match for the will of Christ or the mind of God, which is everlasting. It complicated racial issues and made things confusing. I was bound to be a litigant, and I told them.

Jesus performed quickly and intermittently amid Satan's devilish ruse of power on profane words known to the people of the United States. They seemed to have used the occult or the supernatural in the battle waged. He who knew no sin explained mental illness by having me experience the debilitating faith and fate as a backslider in Christianity. I was thought to be unprotected. So-called professionals who do not understand the color of my skin and my spiritual field of forgiveness, or the lack of it as a drawback, dominated. Eventually, they controlled the mind and emotions of an unspeakable spiritual climate as a believer. I needed the Most High Priest, Jesus, to exorcise me. I believed I was possessed and cursed by the presence and memories of SIU but gifted.

Black militancy brewed and fostered my stance upon my exit from the Railroad. I wanted to assist in solving the Atlanta crimes committed against our youth. The vision in the shrubs of a poorly dressed black male surfaced while I was in a mesmerized state and under surveillance. SIU had broken into my head while they labored relentlessly for me to resign. I felt their method of forcing me out because of the color of my skin was inappropriate. They never mentioned the petty theft. I believed SIU tried to show to thine self be true until I recognized it.

On the other hand, this was not biblical. They had penetrated my mind.

The tumultuous calamities of racism engulfed the sanctity of this African American sister and bred wickedness and militancy. I seized at any given moment retrospective rebellious thoughts of bravery as one who followed the Creator. I perceived their mastermind of a diabolical plan of secrecy confirmed beliefs in what was deceitful and doubtful for me as an honest career as a black public servant. My body was affected by my anger and the undercover operation. Truth, conspiracy, and racism by this profession defected beyond morality as the innocence of my thoughts surged into profanity. The guilt- ridden factors were strong in me. I ran across a bigger white snake in the grass as they forced me out of employment.

Jesus showed within me my true character also. I returned to Christ religiously in 1984, knowing no other help I know. I realized that the war in my head, soul, body, and circumstances had ill equipped me to cope without Him. However, I was still in the world. I continued to do worldly things. I had a relationship with Christ, and I didn't. I was still unemployed and in a sad state of affairs. Reverend Mitchell only taught about black politics and the remission of sins for the justification process in his sermons as I grew up in the Christian faith.

I was a product of prayer in the New York City school system while in the fifth grade, when President Kennedy was assassinated. Weapons kill the body. But they do not destroy the spirit and the soul, which are eternal as a believer.

This is how I won the war against Satan. I used the Word of God and prayed without ceasing until the thought pattern and circumstances changed. Jesus would get rid of the pain of being haunted by their spirits. It was His way of explaining mental illness and racism.

I am an African American female, an offspring of my ancestors who have died for the cost of a free country. They have fought in wars to abolish slavery and racism. Racism is the venom of the accuser who trembles at the Almighty and judges me for my militancy. The Devil is a liar and the father of lies (John 8:44). "For God hath not given us the spirit of fear but of power, and of love, and of a sound mind" (2 Tim. 1:7). Yes, I had a spiritual-warfare problem because of my militancy that was incurred by the white man. I owed no one allegiance but to Jesus. I was a member of the Body of Christ. He allowed these amazing events, yet I had not recovered from my prayers. It was the turning point of my life, and Satan was soon to show his true red, white, and blue colors. I respect and accept people for who they are—black, red, yellow, white, or brown.

This prelude of my young adulthood and first job was devastating because of the color of my skin, my gender—a forgery, a lie, and less than fifty dollars. My employment history marked an ordeal Dr. King and Reverend Mitchell, both of Ebenezer Baptist Church of various locations, would have resolved as problematic from the very acceptance of my inception as a police officer. I could have waited, but I was not thinking. I thought I could handle the job. I felt like I needed the money. Due to my religion, naivety, inhibitions, and insecurities, I was the first black female officer for the freight division in the Bronx forced out. But because of my mistakes on the job, I resigned to allow the company to do whatever they had designed to do without me, their stumbling block. What a relief!

Subsequently the power of prayer changed the stakes after SIU saw that Jesus would perform His mighty works in front of us. "Casting down imaginations and every high thing that exalted itself against the knowledge of God, bringing into captivity every thought to the obedience of Christ, and having a readiness to revenge all disobedience when your obedience is fulfilled" (2 Cor. 10:5-6). My mindset had changed. My faith was tested. With conviction, God allowed me to be whipped mercilessly. I was wicked and antichrist. I had a change of mind from a spiritual high to a sinful worse demeanor. I was out of His will and no longer under the arch of safety. My sins rehashed old wounds which was deep seated. I needed wisdom and deliverance from God. I was a black militant cursed by the devil who was brought to the light in due season. My imagination went wild because I was so pressured, inevitably, our curse manifested into curses. I had a gift from the Holy Ghost worth millions. My God's timing of proving my sanity in this case and the sanctity of it concluded in His wrath. I was unaware of the dangers unforeseen to the human eye, body, soul, and spirit of man that was lurking. Satan had pegged me to reveal the worst in my character in their presence and jeopardized my mental health after disagreeing to the bait of hearing SIU unknown voices. I did not want to be a house n———r. The great white accuser, or Satan, pinpointed me for a lifetime of failure of my God, my family, people, and profession. I became obsessed with SIU and the KKK but rarely looked over my shoulder. My gift was a blessing in disguise. I had no understanding of this righteousness. He wanted me gone.

SPIRITUAL HISTORY BATTLED

*O*n April 30, 1956, in the midnight hour, I was born to battle, being a breech baby. My name is Kim Leslie Smalls, and dedicated back to God to keep a watchful eye on my life in a dedication at Ebenezer, Flushing, New York, officiated by the late Reverend Mitchell. I grew up in the admonition of the Lord under this man of God. I was a member of the Sunday school, the junior choir, the junior usher board, and the junior missionaries. These were the signs of the times we lived in the United States where the Declaration of Independence and the Constitution were based upon Christian principles.

In the sixties, racism prevailed. Wholeheartedly, Reverend Mitchell preached the premise of his sermons each week on politics and government. His black church was heavily into racial, political equality and consciousness as a compelling drive or existing force in his congregation. Regardless, I remained rebellious in my behavior and thoughts. I went down in the watery grave as an innocent disciple and came up a wet, disobedient one. However, I was prompted by Jesus, and I followed.

In my home as well, I remember hearing from the news about Bull Conner from Alabama and Gov. George Wallace. This was the civil rights era, which led our country into her fabric of the civil rights movement. I recall in 1963 when the announcement that President Kennedy was assassinated. Ms. Greenblatt, my fifth-grade teacher, cried like a baby.

I was led by the Holy Spirit to discipleship at the age of seven. As far back as I can remember, the problem of jealousy and domestic violence riddled my family. My mother, who was a devout Christian, would say, "Bob, you're going to make this child sick one day when she grows up." "Death and life is in the power of the tongue" (Prov. 18:21). This was after he had beat her because again he had one too many after a hard day at work as a longshoreman in New Jersey.

Out of their three children, I was the only one awakened out of my sleep by all the commotion in our small two-bedroom apartment in the Woodside Houses. I was the middle child with the middle-child syndrome—not old enough or young enough to be favored in my eyes. I wanted someone to love me. My mom was very strict. I could not wait to leave from under her roof and go to college.

My father was a World War II veteran and a prizefighter from the Navy. I remember he possessed a beautiful shotgun he used for hunting in the woods of his home state of South Carolina. In contrast, my mom was born and raised in Flushing, New York. She had a white aunt, who still resided there. I followed my mom's footsteps into adulthood and prayed for the seed giver of my child to die too. I found out later in life she would take me, unknowingly, to her therapy sessions after work on Fridays.

My dad died on March 26, 1969, when I was only twelve years of age. He had aged tremendously at forty-six, when I had seen him the day before he expired. A year earlier, Dr. King was assassinated on April 4, 1968. As I laid in the Woodhull psych ward in 2008, my history of being raised by my dad was held suspect by my beliefs in Dr. King and his mission. I imagined my dad as the visionary of my flesh who imparted this relationship with a solemn oath to protect Rev. Martin Luther King Jr. prior to his demise. I believed he had prepared his middle child to walk in protective law-enforcement shoes. The police came to eject him regularly from our home.

I could have never succeeded as a police officer due to the fact that I am nearsighted. I could have never have passed at the shooting range in Upstate, New York. I must admit my imagination ran wild about the reason for the violence in the home. Supposedly, my dad guided me to pick up his mantle for the civil rights movement. He fathered a younger child out of wedlock. So money was one factor of arguments in our home. The police in Woodside was called to get me acclimated to being around this type of fraternal order. The vow was if ever anything were to happen to Dr. King, Kim would "pick up his cross and follow" (Mark 10:21). I did want justice to prevail and bring the killer or killers to their knees.

My father was the ultimate provider, and was very protective of his family or anyone who needed help. This delusion answered and reasoned, "Why me?" I believed I could not make heads or tails as to a constant governmental police pursuit. I needed logical answers for the pure speculation in my mind as a schizophrenic. With or without meds, hospitalization and noncompliance of the meds made me more delusional and unsure of my sanity as I contended with Jesus Christ about what He allowed over thirty years because of a "miracle on the tracks."

I was always in the Intellectually Gifted Class (IGC) in elementary school but not very studious as I grew older. I attended Horace Greeley Junior High in the Special Program Enriched (SPE), meaning a three-year program instead of a two-year option for study. I was a latchkey kid. My mom worked as an executive secretary for the Children's Aid Society until retirement. I became a cheerleader in junior high and stayed the course for two years at the New York Institute of Technology. I did have an honors French class in William Cullen Bryant High School. Although I played hooky extensively, I still graduated with an academic diploma. I always showed my intellect among my siblings, but life got the best of me. They succeeded in spite of my high self-esteem and my decline.

I really had no direction. My mom never explained life to me like she disciplined me. My daughter learned from a book. I never contemplated a field of study in high school. I just wanted to attend college like my sister and grad schools. To this day, my college transcript still categorizes me as "undecided" for a major. I followed my own curriculum in social work instead of accounting during orientation because I was called by the Holy Spirit to learn about people. Accounting was my second field of choice, but I minored in Life Science. I did not have an outlook or projection in the field of sociology nor did any research. I trusted Him.

I used illicit drugs as a pastime with my friends in Woodside but never became an addict. I did not have the money to reach an addiction, and I was not a thief. Getting high was for recreation purposes. My mom did her best to keep my mind occupied as a child. I took ballet classes under the direction of Charlotte Pollack Dance Studios from the age of seven to approximately thirteen. Every year, there was a dance recital. Even though I was overweight, I was light on my feet. During the summer months, I went to Darien, Connecticut, under the sponsorship of the Fresh Air Fund for two weeks from seven to thirteen years of age. I continued to revisit the Hock family upon request of the hostess, who was their most gracious representative of the program, consecutively each summer.

I started smoking cigarettes at the age of twelve out of curiosity and wanting to be "grown." My dad smoked. He acquired lung cancer, presumably due to the chemicals and asbestos he was exposed to from his profession and his craft as an auto mechanic. I drank alcohol since junior high school. My girlfriend would bring into class the scotch, milk, and sugar cocktails with tuna fish sandwiches. We sat in the back of the class and indulged as Mr. Green taught math.

The social drinking went on until the new millennium—not unto drunkenness but as a toast to celebrate birthdays only with my mom and family. I stopped smoking in 2001, when cigarettes skyrocketed to a high cost of five dollars a pack. I promised God never to smoke again. I wanted Him to know me as a woman of my word. I had tried on my own unsuccessfully for years. On the lane, we smoked the marijuana. It was easy to chip in for a nickel bag. We called it enjoyment of the nightlife before going to the clubs.

Growing up, there were racial tensions once in a while with Boulevard Gardens, which was predominately white. I always looked at it as good competition in the classroom, especially during spelling bees. I usually won for my class because I read the dictionary somewhat at a very young age in the bathroom, where I was not disturbed.

I started dating at the tender age of fourteen to the best young man or companion I ever had. I was still quite young and wanted to date other people. Albert was furious with me for being so impressionable by all the wrong males, including his cousin. Men were my weakness and ultimately my downfall in life. The first day of college at NYIT, I met the seed giver Festus in Public Speaking class. Unfortunately, he caught my eye too. My mother never bothered to explain life, dating, or my body. I must have played hooky and missed that hygiene class. It was a fatal attraction, and I was hooked. The attraction superseded my better judgment to ever entertain the negro, because that was all he had going for himself of my real interests.

I always wanted to look fine. I had to be possessed to look twice at the male. He wore braids in his hair that he plaited himself and country bumpkin clothes with holes in the knees. He started the trend in 1974. I did not stand a chance. I do not know what I was thinking about. It was the first day of a lifetime of heartache and pain or nightmares. I had plenty of time to think about this in my adult years. But I didn't at seventeen. However, I was not a virgin. My hymen was destroyed by an afternoon fling with a junkie, and I didn't want him. He never explained anything to me about sexual intercourse. Sad to say, that is how I lived my life. I was always a one-night affair or another notch under the belt.

I dated the seed giver from that day almost every day for a semester. He knew how to control his emotions and always blamed me. He had nothing going for himself ever except his ATM card password, which was "God." He never had any money—or so he claimed—and never took me to a movie. I had an active campus life and didn't care. I really can't believe how stupid I was for the male species.

Once I decided to move on, he got derisive because someone else was holding my interest. Festus got wind of it on Hofstra campus and showed in his eyes that he was Satan in the flesh. When I saw the change, I made a mental note of it, but by then, I was hooked. My male friend

Charlie, whom I played Ping-Pong with while Festus was visiting for the first time in Queens, called me up. I was busted and possessed. He had an unhealthy hold on me. He treated me so bad, and I continued to sleep with him. Nothing had changed. He continued to run away from me and slept with other females, and when I finally got rid of the green-eyed monster, he would come back into my arms.

The rejection took a mental toll. So there I was, depressed and pregnant. Overall, years of bed hopping scorned and jaded my wellness in our relationships. I prayed that Jesus would take his life because he quit his job so he would not have to pay the courts for child support. He never gave me any money ever. This was the low life he was leading.

I knew we should have never lived together, but I tried to give Festus a chance. I thought maybe we could reconcile our differences and move on. However, that was short-lived. I came home from work after a midnight tour from the Railroad. I lived in the Queensbridge Houses at the time in New York with my daughter. The apartment looked like a tornado had touched down on it. The dinner plates were still on the living room table with leftover food on them.

I went into the bedroom and woke him up. I needed a babysitter, and he was available. So I hit the roof. I had already made a vow to myself never to marry an alcoholic or become a victim of domestic violence. For the first and last time, he raised his hand at me. I saw the hatred in his eyes again, but the times had changed. I made up in my mind to fight back, and he knew it. He left that night. We permanently broke up again.

He dated other females on purpose or in retribution, and my jealousy seldom ceased to fail me. Festus would find the finest on Adelphi campus where he pledged Alpha or the worst he could find and treat the best. He knew he wasn't bringing anything to the table as a man should. He just continued to sire more children. He knew about my encounter with Dr. King on September 7, 1983.

Annabel, I saw exactly two times in my life. She gave Festus two sons who looked just like him. I wanted my first to be his son and look like him. But God blessed me with a daughter who looks identical to me. Annabel ended up my worst nightmare and enemy to this day. It is utterly ridiculous her spirit has not worn off. In 1985, I started to hear her voice after much pain and agony of artificially induced hallucinations from the oppressors.

I referred Festus to the Railroad. They needed a black male in its ranks for Affirmative Action. I thought possibly he would protect me if we were not on the outs. I believe he let them know I was "possessed." Festus knew they were racist by his responses to me upon applying. I knew him. My so-called relationship cost me a lifetime of degenerates from the male species. Above all, it was too high a price to pay for any overachiever.

My life's journey began in 2000 when I left the male gender to themselves to misuse and abuse. I kept running into criminals. Now I do not care if I never get married. Times have changed. It did not begin with the men in my bed, or did it? This spiritual conflict became as a host of words between my God and their god. The prince of this world, Satan, was dominating in my life because I was not married and was sleeping around. I was a backslider and a whoremonger according to my God.

I landed a school safety officer position, which was a hoax of a job since I was never a hard-core drug addict. I never shot up drugs in my veins. I did not realize the implications of a spiritual stronghold of promiscuity and drugs regarding the deception by the curse of SIU. I thought it happened only in the movies. Eventually, I discovered these white males cursed my life with lies about my God and my faith in Him because of my spiritual strengths and weaknesses. I saw and heard everything in the spiritual world.

My head was haunted by my deceased father's spirit of protection (John 11:11, 23-26) for his child. I knew he was the type of man to awaken out of his eternal sleep for any of his children. No one crosses a Smalls and that be the end of it. My father, in his eternal sleep, awakened in my post office position at the JFK airmail facility while the curse of the Railroad consumed me in monumental animated figures. As a federal employee, I started to hallucinate by seeing icons, which possessed my mind as well as my environment. There was no way of passing the ZMT machine (zip code) tests under the overwhelming odds. The dexterity of my fingers were flawed, and I had not the correct rhythm as my dad looked on. Although I scored over a hundred on the written exam, my anger was infuriated by his presence (Eccles. 9:4-12). While he appeared on their apparatus in his youth and clouded my judgment.

Again, I needed a job and refused to leave. This was prophecy for what was yet to come. I finally resigned six months later to do casework. My supervisors liked the work I produced on Rack 5 and retained me. I dreamed of the Spirit of Jesus Christ by the turbulent sea, the force of a colossal fist with a strong powerful arm of a white man and a gigantic number 7, which means completion in Christianity, with children engraved in it. In hindsight, I had the faith, revelation knowledge, and Holy Ghost power to endure whatever came my way.

I bought a gold wedding band from the pawnshop on Queens Plaza to wear on my forefinger. I lay in my bed and performed a wedding vow as an ordained preacher. In the middle of this nightmare, something or someone haunted my head. I assumed it was a real ring of people who were deceased and angry I had performed this ritual. In my head, I began to feel a wing and development of a glass case. It was like a prism that over the years turned into the movement and colors of a horrific kaleidoscope. Remnants of feathers or a spirit from the dark side still haunted my head. Overall, I assumed I had disturbed someone's beloved. I had made my peace with the angels of heaven except for one that lingered as unforgiving. I do not know what possessed me to do something I thought was harmless. It was another secret.

The early part of 1983, my head was filled with black and white issues. My mind raced with confusion. I was disgusted and sought the Lord's help. The imitation of my cerebellum popped off my head and flew out the bathroom window. I thought this was my soul, which consisted of my mind, will, and emotions. It bothered me and made me uncomfortable. Whatever it was, I was glad that it was gone. However, it seemed to protect my head.

I became a caseworker at Franklin Men's Shelter in the Bronx in 1986. I passed the Supervisor 1, or sup 1 examination but decided to move onward. My coworker hated the job and supervisors who eventually made the shelter become an unhappy place of employment by the city. I took the test for child welfare and started employment in August 1989. I retained the position for nine years. I took my pension money and bought a 1998 Saturn before deciding to relocate to Atlanta, Georgia.

Smoking weed always affected me in a paranoid state of mind. Fortunately, the effects wore off after getting some rest. It gave me a dry mouth and an appetite we called the munchies. It was a pastime in the projects to enhance our idle time in a destructive manner. Peer pressure reared yet again as I followed someone else's lead. My involvement in illicit drug usage of cocaine, marijuana, acid, alcohol, and possibly crack were acts of social stimulation although it was never enough to become addicted. We chipped in and sat on the lane. I resented nodding at the front desk like a heroin addict while employed for School Safety under a nasty curse from SIU. I remember dipping and dabbing with cocaine due to accessibility and availability with my friends from Astoria. It became a pastime. Frequenting church every Sunday and Bible study on Thursdays restrained my drug usage. Slowly, I put down these mind- altering drugs due to the Holy Spirit conviction on life's terms, which were holy and spiritual.

Sam was my high school sweetheart and lover, but he had a cocaine problem. He loved me, but because of family ties, he almost hated Jehovah God. His mom was what they call themselves Jehovah Witnesses watchtower people. Sam and I clashed on this subject, which unknowingly petrified me down by the East River. I don't remember if I was high or not, but Satan possessed him with a horrific appearance that made me run. It was the first and only time such fear gripped me throughout this whole ordeal like that.

When he came to the psych ward to visit, I saw who the visitor was and ran in the opposite direction. I did not want to have anything more to do with him being demon possessed. I saw that Satan was too close for comfort. Besides Festus, Sam was not the only man I knew who had left his jealous lover for me. Knowing Sam, he probably cursed Jehovah God because I actually saw his evil spirit. Besides, we were unequally yoked, and he was in his right mind feeling disdain about the Lord. He had a mouth on him and used profanity often. It could have never been me.

The Railroad's SIU left a spiritual battle of guilt, which eventually escalated into a full-scale war between the Holy Ghost and an evil organization.

THE KING VERSUS THE ANTICHRIST

*T*here was a sudden stillness and peace over the Queensbridge projects on the night of September 7, 1983, at midnight. I looked over at the alarm clock, which read 11:30 p.m. Needless to say, I could not rest. I got up out of my platform bed and went into the living room. I laid on my loveseat.

Suddenly, I heard Reverend Dr. Martin Luther King Jr. say, "I'm happy," and in a voice of the wrath of God. "I want my two million dollars." I had never heard him so angry. A plane flew toward the Fifty-Ninth Street Queensborough Bridge. A white man says, "You son of a b——! I'm not givin you nothin'!" His hatred, disrespect, fear, and guilt sounded like he hastened to make a U-turn and had to press a button to cover up his truths.

A government program shot up in my head from the nape, as a tiny hole appeared in the back of the skull. An animated feature of dogs followed by negatives of gray and black imagery encircled my head. It made a complete circular formation while bursting in my sight. The second circling ended with a piece of steel lodged in my left temple. The nature of this program was hostile to me, seeing it was to hide and protect a crime.

Dr. King knew this white man as a perpetrator he had fallen victim to in his mortal state of being. Dr. King, in his final hours, was supposedly protected by the Federal Bureau of Investigation. I believed the white man blew his own cover for reasons unknown. A basic in law enforcement is to cover your butt. He was an enemy to Reverend King. So I too was his enemy. This time, I did not mind following the leader. The white man's plane was equipped with a federal government program manufactured in their laboratory to conceal information and/ or if necessary cover themselves.

I reacted with elation that Dr. King was a guardian angel of mine, "for He shall give angels charge over thee, to keep thee in all thy ways" (Ps. 91:11, Luke 24:23). Just for the moment, I felt protected for a little while as he became my mentor. Why did God wake up this civil rights leader from out of his eternal sleep? What was this messenger from God implicating and insinuating? What was the meaning of all my visions? Was it blood money, because Dr. King never lived the life of a millionaire? He gave his money away. Was there a KKK contract on his life? Why was there a white man in a casket while Dr. King stood at attention in my vision? What was the Savior saying? Why was reverse psychology used to empower their fear, oversee, and implement acts of terrorism and haunting? I thought. The speculations surmounted immensely as I always pondered over government involvement in his death. Was there a two- million dollar contract on his life? In my opinion, the government always knows more than the general public, like Malcolm X, who also had FBI problems.

I was honored by Dr. King's presence and perceived him to be on the level of Jesus Christ. Then it dawned on me: they knew who I was. I felt I was in a life-and-death situation. But little did I know. I was promoted to detective. I had no clue as to how I was going to get out alive. I was in a state of shock.

I said, "Jesus, what you do that for? You know they are going to kill me."

At that instant, I saw Reverend King in a vision, standing erect, with a black handkerchief tied around his face like he was a thief in the night. "The thief cometh not, but for to steal, and to kill, and to destroy" (John 10:10). From that moment on until the new millennium, there was a transference of thought in psychiatry "motherf———r" that arose from a deep place in my mind. It was not my own thought. Yet it was in my head. I was fully aware of what was going on. After much conscience preponderance of thought, I realized I was a mere bystander, a witness, and did not take part in the occurrence (Acts 4:20). It was like the white man had something else on his mind. He sent it, and I read it.

For years, I carried the guilt of profanity being my thought. Then finally, I realized I could never interfere with anything between Dr. King and this man at that time. Secretly, I thought the white man from the plane proved himself as he threatened my life by his ungodly thoughts and deeds. Transference is when the accuser accuses his victim instead of accepting his own responsibility for the profanity in this case. I was of a childish innocence in their presence and had not any profane remark.

I gave a deathbed request, or what I thought to be a calling of a near-death experience. I always wanted to marry, and saw in another vision Mr. and Mrs. Martin Luther King Jr. standing side by side. Then from street level, or Vernon Boulevard, I heard in a loud, clear voice, "You better not cross that white man!"

The sellout, knew him. I thought he could have appeared from the Army because an Army veteran lover, now a corrections officer in the spiritual realm, requested me to be disloyal to Rev. King. I refused with a resounding no.

Paraphrasing scripture, what profit a man to gain the whole world and to lose his own soul? (Luke 9:25) In addition, I knew better, although I didn't know scriptures at this time.

Nevertheless, Rev. King stood up again in another vision and looked like he was overseeing things. The white man was authorized by someone to oversee me. But he was infringing upon my space at my home and in my head. I believed reverse psychology in the last vision I noted: seeing a white man in a casket with a gray bushy mustache and a partially bald head. That was the last time Dr. King was seen in his shell or his body in a casket by the public. I then decided to get some sleep, and like a baby, I did rest. I had no idea what to expect the very next day or over the next twenty to thirty years.

As I reflected, I saw my life was in for a big change. The only police I knew was SIU and the Federal Bureau of Investigation, like Dr. King did. I believed because they had a government program. It was the FBI. Will the real King assassin please stand up from sanity to insanity?

After much thought, I decided to tell no one. I did not realize that the plan of his guilt-ridden status would cost me my sanity and a lifetime diagnosis of a serious mental illness, which varied among numerous doctors over a course of thirty years. It was a psychotic reverse psychology, social, psychological, sociopathic, spiritual cover-up by the enemy—a classic concept. A concept I have seen before in a movie, like the Mission Impossible series. I became a literal enemy of the state.

Ronald Reagan was the president at this time. I do not believe any president knew about this. However, I believed someone in management did. I thought the FBI spent an astronomical amount on the imagination of a great white hope of the KKK to box with God. It could have been two million dollars. And so, the holy war for me had just begun.

I never knew God would use me in such a tremendous assignment of being a black female alone in a battle with the FBI, with racists, or with the US Army in the background. It was pretty big. I thought, if I made my bed in hell, He will be there (Ps. 139:8), and so He was. There are consequences for sin. On the other hand, I worship a risen Savior who was on my side. He promised to never leave me nor forsake me (Heb. 13.5). He washed me whiter than snow in the interim (Isa.1:15). Moreover, I became a new creature in Christ (2 Cor. 5:17). I was working out my soul salvation with Jesus. I was in the clear.

Unfortunately, I believed I became a government scapegoat and their distraction for the real issue of FBI monetary use.

Jesus continued to strengthen and bolster my faith through His presence and His grace. His never-ending love for me anchored in my heart, and His protection hovered closely on the horizon. I believed the crimes of the century had yet to be solved totally and truthfully, but maybe on God's calendar. I believed this accomplishment was still a mystery on what really happened in the death and investigation of King. I thought reciprocity of due diligence in a grief-stricken state of this world by the Most High God is assuredly a way of acknowledgment and a welcome touch by His mighty hand living in racist America. The judicial system of inequality wanes governing the rights of the masses under a presidential mockery of freedom and justice. Political pressures have made it remote for a minority to govern effectively stunting the growth of racial equality and law enforcement.

Reverend King inspired me to reach a height and depth of moral excellence, portrayed by Jesus Christ as a model of His Father for this world (John 10:30). Dr. King depicted a father figure of this caliber I had missed growing up in the projects. He was a mental giant whom in all his genius displayed a life I did not emulate as a twenty-seven-year-old disciple by exemplary conduct as Jesus, the Son of the Living God and the Son of Man.

Dr. King embraced this sinful sick soul and his love for me by eventually paving my Christian road on a journey that supported life and victory. His sustained vision of repentance as a wholesome woman and a detective of peace- officer status in cracking this case by an African American female were compelling. I know that the white man was a killer because he tried to kill me for years. I believed it was blood money and the terms of a contract they knew who ordered Reverend King's demise and my haunting.

The aftermath of knowing that your own country avenged your life for money, politics, power, and racism influenced me into a version of the Antichrist by a defeated foe. I knew immediately I had won this case as a lawyer. My privacy was invaded. On the other hand, I was in for the fight of my life as a litigant. I believed to arrange a war between Jesus Christ and the law enforcement of the United States of America was painstakingly far short of an immediate loss by this organization.

"For we wrestle not against flesh and blood, but against principalities, against powers, against the rulers of the darkness of this world, against spiritual wickedness in high places" (Eph. 6:12). As they relentlessly attempted to slay me regardless of whom God is in this world and His meaning to the masses as Creator, I survived. Dr. King's assassination was a crime perpetrated by a loser and by others perceived as hero. So "they" say. It seems hard to believe a two- bit loser like James Earl Ray can outsmart and outshine the famous FBI even after someone tampered with the crime scene, as per Soledad O'Brien (CNN).

To think Jesus would not subject this country to judgment is ludicrous for this male servant and the Body of Christ. To unsuccessfully attempt to think of outsmarting the Creator on a rebound costs vast amounts of convincing, power, and lifetime. It just can't be done. In my opinion, the degree of cost taxpayers remit for transparency by all parties involved in this insane schism does not suffice a deathbed confession by a lone unknown. Not less when a perpetrator of his own guilt is at large and accused by his own victim actions of a mysterious crime in 1983. This occurrence is the reason for my diagnosis.

Today was another day of reckoning. The judgment of the Almighty God El Shaddai Jehovah will allow Satan to fixate the level of darkness, as I look forward to the circuit of what goes around, comes around. I perceived His Son had rule, dominion, and all power prevailing against the stench of these G- men who manage the grounds of the United States with a John Wayne syndrome. These rights are contractual by the Constitution of the people. They require sound wisdom of authority to most men, women, and those confused about their sexuality of lifestyle, according to the Bible.

"No weapon formed against me shall prosper…and every tongue that shall rise against thee in judgment thou shall condemn" (Isa. 54:17). "My people perish for the lack of knowledge" (Hosea 4:6). To those who oppose terrorist- government foolishness, this terror plot cosigns a period of unrest in the nation of Islam, Black Panthers, and civil discord of my people. Jesus does laugh. Discourse is seemingly plentiful in the people of color due to civil rights issues, injustices, and character assassination by law enforcers due to cover-ups by withdrawals of good judgment, imagination, and phobia. I believed this century wearies us all of quagmire battleground tactics, like so-called weapons of mass destruction and arbitration pursued in the streets of passage by the flawed justice system.

Beware of the memories of ancestral people from the outhouse to the White House who farm the pleasures of white sick people in their subhuman thought patterns who degrade our existence as below humankind. My blood is still red, even to a people who would bear the burden with their ghastly association to the white race. I believed KKK confederates farm or cultivate outlandish styles of killing my people and wonder why we fight for equality, peace, justice, and freedom in the United States.

Times have changed. I believed the offspring of this racist policing frighten with perilous fits of rage and supernatural powers of darkness affiliated with the wheels of tension and injustices, which invade my privacy. In my opinion, thought-provoking mind-sets that warn law enforcers and military might of 9/11 failures will not cease to accept reaping what you sow (Gal. 6:7) for their acts of corruption of my environment because of racism, power, money, or a mystery.

My black life does matter to my God. Hipsters who join knee bends and challenge my mental wellness or power and inflict harmful ideas because of my being of natural color in mankind are sadistic. I thought the Pentagon ran into the hills with jet-flamed pieces of iron, which undoubtedly curtailed them all into a quivering stance urging humanity to avenge this land. This terror encompasses the fear of God and awes his children. White-male dominated chauvinistic departments in politics, law enforcement, and the military of danger and despair as warring characters because of religion, power, racism, and money in this country are a sign of the times. Jesus is a Holy God (Lev. 11:45) who is dedicated to his church and projects life in my plight to overcome the profanity, fanciful, frenzy of zany speech covering meant by the federal organization to kill, curse, and demonize me.

Profanity in my hearing can make a person sick as a result of their theme.

In 2013, I learned their profane response to Dr. King as their mission statement. The deceptive patterns deviate into troubled waters, which, shipwrecked by the sands of time and my frantic mustering of bravery, is faith filled (2 Tim. 1:7). The sell-outs' sense of fear encompasses the faith in the white man and their intrinsic past—determined as illusive, inanimate characters in high places led by racists—succumbed to this harmful law enforcement mentality. Then Satan awaits finality of work each day as he rants in retirement of the night, threatening my living as a gaping hole in the pit of hell's fire due to my power, his expletives, the use of his money, sexual encounters, and the color of my skin.

In my opinion, Dr. King made it explicitly obvious about the Federal Bureau of Investigation's theft or contract of his mysterious two million dollars. I wait for the time of fear, despair, and despondency in their life of terrorism as a brute force unable to attain success in their efforts to cover up their deficiencies. This is why they run around the United States and overseas to apprehend terrorists today. You reaped what you sowed and subjected us all to the threat of terrorism avenged by the Almighty.

I am more than a conqueror (Rom. 8:37). I believed these factions muster up somber wavelengths and sexual communication lines that roll upon the shores of thunderous tides, which display roaring reams of guilt-ridden tenacity in a profane theme. It is so bitterly overcome with heights, barren of any positive energy and light. I thought these professionals and coconspirators of workaholic measures tip the scale of the civil rights movement by apathetic rides of pigeon planes jetting their way to adulterous, lewd descent into profanity and in my bed.

Their practice declined into unbearable sustenance by their Satanic spirits, where demonizing the Satanic negro creep eerily in the mind of violence by their use of money and personnel. They want unjust rewards set forth toward me to die a gruesome death by natural causes because I am not one of theirs.

The demonic law enforcement in my head sought to scare me to death. I believed they wanted the comfort of witchcraft by their hot blood to use curses and sex with their supernatural power to overcome me.

The awe of Satan reached far beyond the scope of motherhood in female drops of blood. I believed females of witchcraft in blustery winds of adamant sexism and the gift of gab I cite as spirits of danger. In my opinion, their need of intentional glory for ungodly worship by abominations for their attempts to kill and by assault was imminent. The horrific psychological warfare of hate bearing all seeds through the matters of the heart and exposes the ill-fated taxed victor of subjective speech patterns of profanity. I thought their speech has serious vulgar implications of unrest, unjust jargon below the belt by this abnormal encounter. I believed this breeding ground unscrupulously asserted the tension-driven force of systemic foreplay by capacity of fornication, marital sex, lying, profanity, and cursing.

I set up house with Trevor for eleven years during this ordeal. He would hold my head as treachery of combat filled my mind with hate, profanity, and sex. In due season, the Holy Spirit ran him away. I grew stronger in my faith.

I believed the culprits rely for future reference into a pit of fire and lustful hazardous styles of cheap female ventures masterminding laborious efforts in our sexual activities in their sky writing. Sheer words express the spirit of destruction by the sex of immoral distractions throughout this war of words and assault by adulterers on this fornicator. This supernatural operation of assault emerges the rights of passage from the womb cantankerously vile mishaps of joining together with grief in the air.

I thought it sounded like my female counterpart had been enveloped into crevices of deep depression by darkness, as she solemnly devotes to her cue in voice and reactions to the leader. I believed she was his cover and partner for my demise. I remembered when his cover was blown. I thought she had to respond to his sociopathic sexual foul play and admit to this action. I could hear the whispers, which are eventually disclosed covering up their plot, his anger, and their sex life. He shouts and gets obnoxious when I win my point, when they are in error, and when there is something he does not want to be said or done. He covers with an attack or assault to my head and body.

I planned to relocate to Chicago or Detroit the next day, although I was tricked. I believed the FBI coaxed me into a spiritual possession by advisement of what to keep and discard from my personal effects as they supernaturally surrounded me. I thought they used this as a distraction.

I remembered again to "love your enemies" (Matt. 5:44), so I was, for the most part, compliant. I did have a mind of my own, which didn't last long.

On the first stop in Chicago, I started to hallucinate. Figures of African witchcraft and sorcerous images reared their ugly heads from the pit of unsavory curses, profanity, and black magic. Profanity bewitched as I struggled to stop my mind from racing, knowing it was due to artificially induced symptoms by our secrets from who I thought was the Federal Bureau of Investigation. I did not anticipate nor realize the harm, hurt, or danger in maneuvers and implementation by powers of darkness, or the black arts, from a rogue law enforcement outfit at this time immediately overhead through the occult. I believed the atmosphere was charged and permeated by government voices as they encircled my being, performing a séance. I felt they conspired to kill, possess, or urge me to commit suicide because of the darkness of their supernatural power in our sexual conduct and their marriages. They said they were hiding behind "the rings on their finger" and our promiscuous lifestyles.

On April 7, 2013, I saw the King assassination on CNN once again as commentated by Soledad O'Brien. I was set up for embarrassing moments and assault throughout the course of twenty years of hell on earth. My walk with God was not yet straight and narrow (Matt. 7:4). However, I was driven by the Holy Spirit to survive. Dr. King had a marriage made in heaven, and I was the whore of regret. I believed the FBI stole my soul by cursing my emotions, mind, and memories. Unknowingly, I was set on a path of unforeseeable mountain of misery by witchcraft, as seen in a dream even though I could not be plucked out of the Master's hand (John 10:28-29). Sometimes, I lived my life regardless of the scrutiny, restraints, and the haunting by the Federal Bureau of Investigation's presence.

I thought I needed the comfort and protection of a man in my life. If only I could feel Jesus hold me, and I prayed about this type of comfort. My dreams were spiritual nightmares that foretold the future. He did not want me to live in sin. They continued to treat me like a thing. What was invisible to the naked eye or the spiritual realm was visible to me as the spirit of Satan ran loose in my head. The normal minds of men cannot fathom the white man's abomination for God, Dr. King, and my Christian way with the Lord. I believed promiscuity and the supernatural were two of my major problems with the Feds as their profanity stayed at the tip of their tongues in my mind.

Detroit was a release from the past, or so I believed, as I lay in my newly carpeted apartment I rented. The thoughts of my entire life passed through my mind as they physically made their appearance and haunted my body, soul, and spirit. After that occurrence, I left the apartment and got into my vehicle. I needed to escape from life. Escapism was always a vent for me in my bed. I had a problem that vied for my attention, and I wanted it solved, even if it took me over thirty years to resolve with the assistance of my Savior, of course.

As I sat in my car, a white-speckled-with-pink prehistoric animal pierced the windshield without shattering the glass. With its great nozzle head, it nudged me on the forehead twice before becoming hostile. I pondered how I was going to get out of this. Apparently, when it became aggressive, I drew back in defense. I was ready to fight. Then I saw a beautiful angel or spiritual being dab on the front of the hood of the vehicle twice with her forefinger before disappearing with her staff.

I felt the clandestine operation of guilt-ridden hysteria and as the Great Accuser or Master of Confusion saw fit to follow my every move by cunningly tampering with me, temporarily ridding my mind of all thoughts of normalcy of my past in brainwashing and whitewashing by a battery of lies, expletives, or more distractions. I believed they conjured up events, overlapped events, and lifted dangerous underworld prehistoric beasts. They forced methods of destroying my sinful actions of youthful endeavors to substantiate their claims for my treason. They said.

Every day that God sent was filled with a bombastic, eerie feel of primitive warlike creatures and curses of monumental capacity of proportions eating at my skin. I nearly passed out coming home from Detroit when I was attacked by the "birds." I shun thoughts about any other animal, such as rats. They picked at my brain until I almost collapsed at the wheel of my car on Route 80. Overall, I had to walk and not faint (2 Cor. 5:7). Stubbornly and rebelliously, I refused to pray. But Jesus stopped the attack by his infinite wisdom, grace, and mercy.

After surviving the ride to New York, I suffered on a daily basis the workings of the Antichrist. The white man from the plane kept repeating to me that this was "his job." They wrote themselves up as being "our Father which art in heaven" (Matt. 6:9) and Festus as Jesus Christ. The gall and assault by words of sexual encounters I endured when I decided to pray to Jesus were overwhelming. Slowly, I unraveled the scheme. The plan was orally acknowledged and dissipated, which made them even angrier. I had to endure to the end and stumble upon most of the whole plot. I heard the Feds' mission statement or theme was "F——k you, motherf——ker!"

"Weeping may endure for a night, but joy cometh in the morning" (Ps. 30:5). Morning did not come anytime soon. I suffered like a biblical character and book named Job, who was a righteous man of God. Satan just could not only kill him but also had free reign over his life and everything that he owned.

Their words carried the black arts of demonic powers in the occult.

One particular night late in November of 1983, I remembered being coiled by a boa constrictor, I thought, which nearly killed me. I knocked hard on heaven's door with a whole heart of faith whereas all that is necessary is a mustard seed to cast the mountain into the sea (Matt. 17:20). This was when I realized they were trying to kill me, and I needed my God. The ordeal has been a close call or brush with death and unjust insanity claims in heavenly places at the throne of grace. It was surrounding sounds and actions by the Antichrist.

Their actions and speech proved to me they hated God. It was unjust claims of schizophrenia, the paranoid type. It is followed by a supernatural and spiritual win in favor of my spiritual litigation. Jesus had to intervene. He is the Just One who loves justice.

This was the unjust work of the supernatural, Mother Nature in her prime. It has been a lull of great pain as they have shown penis-driven acts by animated archangels of royalty from the depths of turmoil. Harvard's minority listing wanted me for special education, not criminology. Their insane criminal acts upon ludicrous assumptions by my black power are in epidermis relations and the affairs of a fiendish money scandal. My power comes from above given by Jesus through the Holy Ghost not because of the color of my skin but because of a murder mystery, or a so-called theft agreement. I already experienced the supernatural that filled my heart with the Spirit of God.

I was anointed for this assignment. The black arts of darkness dropped a dead featherlike remains of a pigeon or a rat from my heart. Its aftermath from the snake and my faith dropped into the pit of my abdomen as time lapsed into another month. I could feel the feathers or the fur. I did not have a clue that voodoo was utilized to unnerve me as the accumulation of African sorcery put me in a state of shock. I identified the African black arts from the movies.

The demonic force of the false prophet gripped the white man from the plane. I heard his voice. But on occasion, God would show me a monumental figurine that hovered over Long Island City. He showed me that the serpent in its resting place was symbolic of Satan.

One evening, which was typical for me to be under attack, I envisioned an East Indian man sitting with his legs crossed inciting a séance, trance, or spell through an incantation. I was in my bedroom, and he was in the corner of my living room ceiling, chanting. It sounded as if the white man was in the hallway stairwell when I heard his mom say, "Son?" This was a spiritual journey that woke up his mother from her eternal sleep. He had a childlike respect for someone. Every now and then, I got chances to instigate the severe, dangerous mockery of their life-and-death situations. Jesus weighed His judgment on their fiendish, eerie, and cruel actions.

The enemy would then regroup and retaliate by attacking me all at once with black magic, which was much more powerful than first thought. It was immensely heinous, eerie, and overwhelming. I believed they were hell bound and infuriated, hostile, or livid about my jest. I understood they did not like their own medicine, and put me in a state of shock by a complete nervous breakdown.

However, when God supernaturally smote them or took some kind of recourse, I became the villain. I believed his mom caused such an earth- shattering glass appearance that she penetrated my entire body. The thrilling effects were seeking refuge, which was hysterical in laughter and in gloom. It was funny to know that this devilish man could be so boyish by his mom. But her response was chilling and very uncomfortable for me as well.

The demonic spirit effected my body by design. My head was the main target of horrifying black arts or powers of darkness and maneuvers by the government agency. I told Trevor it was my head I needed him to hold and caress. The satanic possession was that of artificial symptoms induced, which consisted of hearing voices, the racing thoughts of profanity, seeing the spiritual realm, telling lies, and feeling the evil spirits (demons) at work by the occult. I learned how to use my sword, which is the Word of God and faith, in death-defying insane circumstances of everyday life and living with this monster.

The ruse of having a permanent mental illness grew worse as the years evolved. I believed they whitewashed and brainwashed my mind of normal thought patterns. In my opinion, I had to prove that this demonic possession by the law enforcement agency was insane to God too and had nothing to do with sex. Trevor and I were not ready for marriage.

I perceived the fright, flight spiritually navigated in and beyond the unknown to a place of tranquility with curses from the mind and lips of a killer. I bear witness to the deceptive vices of artificial symptoms induced through criminal acts of entering the human mind and brain by insane, immoral drives of horrific, ghastly scenes and war-torn pain while I focused on prayer. I can only tell about the impact it had on my life and body, the eternal sleep of Dr. King and my dad, their actions, and that which was revealed by the Spirit of the Living God. In the heavens was a twisted curl of air with expletives that saturated the heavens as I attempted to pray. It was filled with profanity in the earthly realm and serious repercussions of assault.

I believed the FBI flipped the script through distractions and had me so furious with heaven that their air curl of profanity was a consequence of my waking hours if I got any sleep that day. One night, while under attack, I saw and felt a blue index finger touch my forehead and immediately put me to sleep. I had not slept in days. I was the only one calling on the name of the Lord, and the next thing I knew, I was asleep. Unfortunately, my prayers had to go through the first and second heavens of expletives before reaching the throne of grace or the kingdom of God. I needed Jesus to decipher through the profanity in the spiritual realm the words from my heart. There was so much pain in the skywriting I decided to gather evidence and take it to the United Nations for justice to be served.

My mother lived in close proximity to LaGuardia Airport. She caught me collecting signatures of those complaining about the noise pollution day in and day out. My mother and sister decided at best to send me to the psych ward of Elmhurst Hospital. I was handcuffed like a common criminal. I told the attending physician about my September 7, 1983, experience. My family did not see it fitting to contact Reverend Mitchell. I truly needed to know about spiritual warfare after fully coming back to Christ years later.

I had a praying mom. We knew if we touched and agreed on a divine healing, it shall be so. No matter how long it took, God has to answer prayer. It is a promise and the groundwork of His salvation plan for me. However, it was a subject taboo to the Baptist faith and one seldom wanted to undertake. I could not explain then the ordeal as a spiritual problem of acceptance to a team of scientists. My family had me committed. I thought my mind was challenged henceforth with secrets that could not be divulged due to their nature and the unfathomable works by the Federal Bureau of Investigation. I learned another lesson, but it was too late.

The very air I breathe carried so much witchcraft and sorcery that the synthetic, plastic air pocket popped in my mouth as I spoke. It would attack my head first and proceed out of my mouth as I inhaled and exhaled. The black magic was full of curses, accusations, deception, gall, guile, distractions, and guilt about my past that the excruciating pain in the human body turned asunder its deviance into normal thought construct and natural systems as horrifying. The respiratory and blood circulation properties, mixed with venom, endangered my wellness mentally, physically, emotionally, and spiritually for twenty years nonstop or feeling of every waking minute. The pollutants of artificial instincts affected my excretion system simply because I am human. I was attacked and became man-made as if I was a thing. I constantly called on the Lord. Scripture says He chastens those He loves (Heb. 12:6). When my promiscuity came to an end, the assault stopped, but I had to go through what was already written up.

By this time, I believed the white man and his followers were criminally insane in the spiritual realm. They were admitted sociopaths. I always contended with the Most High God that one and one equals two and the rest was pure insanity. Above all, the laws of nature were broken not only with the death of King. The F word became a part of my solemn thoughts of sound and clear judgment. Jehovah God, our Father, reminds me to this day. He will always be a Holy God who should be reverenced, and I agreed. I fought for thirty years for a normal, peaceful mind (Gal. 5:22). One who had the free will to love and choose God for the life of deliverance by my Lord and Savior, Jesus Christ, the Anointed. I cared to revere the Lord and to serve Him as "the truth shall make me free and when Jesus sets me free. I shall be free indeed" (John 8:32, 36).

I tried everything I could think possible to cease from troubling. The peace of God, which passes all understanding (Phil. 4:7), eventually solved all these problems. Mental, emotional, physical, and spiritual concepts of life followed a normal path of righteousness of God as the body, soul, and spirit of man evolved forward in Christianity. I had to shed the black arts of paranormal supernatural darkness and power, as noted by Stacey Jones from Central New York Ghost Hunters. Eventually, I had to get fully dressed in my war clothes. I had my helmet of salvation on, my breastplate of righteousness, my shield of faith, my loins girded with the truth, my feet shod with the gospel of peace, and my sword of the spirit, which was the Word of God (Eph. 6:14-17).

Once upon a time, I shook like a leaf in the cold winds of winter from the heinous circumstances of simply my head upon my shoulders. My God gradually repaired the trauma to my nervous system. The sternum flapped repulsively as voices jeered the operation of an unholy war underneath my breath. Now my tremors are due to the meds. As I closed my eyes, I could see the fright of the FBI entering in by way of the right side of the base of the brain as their words circled to the left hemisphere to the temple. The mention of cancer would permeate the walls of the abdomen while the pain shot through the entire body. Another point of entry through the vocal cords vibrated as a miniature snake appeared and tunneled its way into my hypothalamus. It was soul stirring as well as soul wrenching.

After designing the head to the bodily functions, solace could only be found in the Word of God through prayer, praise, fasting, and worship. I dropped out of sight. I thought I was no longer on enemy radar after he was through with me for that day. Impossibilities had been endured as I overcame their pain to the end of the assault. The deception induced a rage and range of emotions, which had to be perfect or they would replay the thought pattern until my prayers translated expletives to the Lord. It was as if I was some kind of tape recorder. They wanted me to stop communicating with Jesus. I could hear the white man utter and insist this was "his job" while the assault battered as he barraged me with our sins.

Their witchcraft and sorcery would settle on my skin and eat me alive. I was simply terrorized and traumatized by their truths, guilt, and fear. They featured Anabel and her insanities as a buffoon with extraordinary intelligence and equated her with the white man. I believed the FBI animated a group of Kings with crowns and robes majestically attired with an erection while their penis was exposed. I could see the dogs drooling at the mouth as the attack worsened. My thought patterns constricted my mind to terrorism. I knew Satan as a defeated foe after reassuring myself that justice will prevail in the long run. During my menstrual cycle, the curse of expletives would drop onto the pad and eat my flesh as words of bloodthirsty savage beasts dropped from my head. I continued to pray and repent.

Satan and the thought of Jesus Christ in my bed emerged as I fornicated.

The pain was so unbearable. Having worked in the mental health field, I knew these sacrilegious acts were not uncommon to females. The males vented their anger at Him by expletives as well. Consequently, all my sins were accounted for while living through an outdated Old Testament law. Jesus brought the two greatest commandments: one, "to love the Lord thy God with all your heart, soul, mind," and strength and two, "to love thy neighbor as thyself" (Matt. 22:37-39). Satan insisted upon accusing me of my sinful lifestyle and whatever was not like God, the Father, Son, and Holy Spirit. I maintained my innocence of any wrongdoing I thought during this federal probe and saga. Who were they to judge?

Jesus revealed how they were obsessed by their annulling of history. He showed me and slowed the clock in the mid-eighties to a near standstill. I almost collapsed in the present, which had a future. In my opinion, the Feds wanted to annihilate the world of words to smite King Jesus and this mighty man of the cloth. With the little secret briefcase, they pressed the detonator. But on a sure foundation, they shook the world I was living in. The vision disclosed I had the weight of the world physically and spiritually on my shoulders. It was extremely heavy. I believed I was in the last minute of light and life. God exemplified and literally equated me in a vision as Atlas, the Greek Titan. Then He sped up time.

My Christian experience immensely built up my confidence, love, trust, courage, and, last but not least, my faith in God. He revealed sorcerous minds of ungodly satanic and subhuman orders of an adult form that hatched its hatred upon the world. The great accusers in my innocence had me guilt ridden about my lifestyle, sins, and past. As a newly born-again believer, I knew nothing of the extent of Satan's powerful wiles and his irrational, insane ruse as related to the norms of the land. He did not care. I believed the white man and Anabel thought of anything and everything sick, which was said to have happen in the spirit world.

I would dream of Jesus and His vigilance before the King occurrence. However, I could not interpret His message. My mind told me of another planet that was looking at the assault and violence year after year. I remember the female leader telling me if I ever needed any witnesses they would be glad to testify. They explained that the reason they did not assist was because they are a peaceful planet and have no weapons. It sounded like heaven to me.

I believed their attempt to asunder my spirit, body, and soul from God totally violated the life of John and the law of repentance in the Christian faith. It was unbearable to relive my lifestyle at twenty-four. It was unthinkable and unimaginable the time spent in the household of faith to see this sort of outcome. They were still the defeated foe regardless of my backslidden condition, the war waged against me, and the select few of this divine caliber. Trevor had to go. This was a war waged against the leader of the civil rights movement, a child of God and King Jesus by the Antichrist, or the false prophet.

There were times I felt I was a mother to Jesus. I felt so bad for Him, like He was my Son. He didn't deserve the hatred. It was due to my maternal instincts at work. He did not have to take the abuse we went through together although the chastisement of my peace was upon Him (Isa. 53:5).

Knowing Satan as the master of confusion and the destroyer of life as we know it, his presence interrupted my child's nurturing for the sake of the Body of Christ. I put my daughter in Jesus's hands as Guardian. Yes, I had strayed away from my Christian upbringing that Jesus permitted by this great assignment. She had suffered enough. She did not live with me. My mom had custody of her for educational purposes. I did know my Deliverer and breakthrough by the Holy Spirit was hanging in the balance of their love for me.

I diligently sought the Lord for expediency on this complicated matter. I believed the Feds seized over twenty years of heartaches by mindless violence against an innocent civilian and the elect of Christ. In 1984, I wrote the United Nations about Dr. King and every ethnic newspaper I could get my hands on in the "melting pot" of Queens. I sang gospel in front of the UN and gave a copy to one of the Middle Eastern diplomats as she approached security. I passed it to her driver, and five minutes later, her male employee came running outside as I looked back for acknowledgment.

I joined a community church in Astoria and began to learn about spiritual warfare, demons, and Satan every chance I got. Nevertheless, it was unwelcome in the House of the Lord. None of the pastors in thirty years wanted to tackle the black craft or powers of darkness. Society had this problem of assassination for centuries like the black arts, and it is evident today the perpetrators have a lineage of sociopathic offspring due to power, politics, and color.

I got fatigued and tired of being sick and tired. I called out the man whom I believed was the FBI supervisor, or some kind of higher-up. But he failed to make an appearance on Vernon Boulevard. I went to church clad with my youthful usher attire. I met the pastor at church. We did not get a chance to converse because he had a business appointment. So I returned home to Queensbridge. I was going to usher them to hell as gatekeeper. I ran into females who resembled friends of the prettiest angel, Lucifer, once known as in heaven before He got expelled. I knew if Jesus lived on this planet today, law enforcement would follow him and gun him down like a dog on sight because of his power and his principles.

The depression of being shot supernaturally continued in the head, leaving misery and pain and draining me of my positive energy. My energy was sapped, and I was burned out. That night, there was a shot in the hallway as I lay in bed in my sixth-floor apartment. I went to the door. I peered through the peephole. I saw nothing and backed up. Out of my belly came a spiritual bullet. Planes flew overhead through an abyss of darkness in the night. There was death-defying days by these devilish upsets.

After I unraveled the mystery hidden in the interwoven bands of air pockets, I found it was thought provoking, and a level head prevailed against the spirits from behind the scenes. As mysteries unfolded, Satan would attack and distract another area of the left hemisphere of my brain. After two decades of excruciating pain and torture to the body, I thought the Feds had run out of ideas on how to outsmart the Most High God, or was it the right dosage of Haldol? I believed I assented to medicate periodically anything having to do with governmental or spiritual work by their lord or the enemy if it is going to touch me. They stole my thoughts, ideas, memories, and emotions and cursed me as I strove to better myself through Jesus's saving grace.

To live for Jesus meant He had to make me over. I had a new outlook to emulate as a new creation in Christ. My mind was renewed by the corrections of lifestyle, which eliminated bed hopping and going to the clubs. I had a problem of profanity in my mind when I was angry. I believed that was corrected first by the Federal Bureau of Investigation. I repeatedly had to repent for a slip of the mind. Under the attack, it was inevitable, and I was bound to fail by design. Throughout their assault of expletives, I did not cuss most of the time, but that is what they did not want me to think. The start of the profanity of choice words and their theme or mission statement was ill.

I was just trying to find my soul mate instead of the Christian way of him finding me. It seemed I first had to respect my own body for someone to respect me, after twenty years of bondage in government, which ran amok. Lulled by the Haldol that I thought was taking out my hair; it could have been a possible side effect. The dermatologist informed me there was no evidence of this being true. It was the process of getting older and the harsh treatment of chemicals that stopped my consumption of this medication. It was an excuse for the enemy to conjure up other demonic devices of trickery, deception, and disrespect for human life. Only Haldol got rid of all the symptoms. In 2015, it makes me paranoid it had been going on since before the turn of the century. So I still can become delusional. But the doctor is satisfied. I'm not.

The depraved mind of callous gist cared less about treating me like a thing.

The attacks racked my entire body, from the soles of my feet to the crown of my head. I was beaten so much by spiritual wickedness in high places and the powers of darkness that I became somewhat immune to the physical effects. Nevertheless, I still had a human body that longed to be caressed. I thought the Feds frequently battered my mind with fright to no anticipated relief. The pain would subside every now and again tremendously as I prayed for alleviation from the ground war. I asked God then to never let me die a violent death and to rapture. However, it was not time for either.

I continued to correspond with the United Nations and other media for self-protection and prevention by merciless law enforcers. I thought the Feds could not shut down the will of His government-related awesome circumstances. Jesus was sanctifying me into a new creation of His kingdom. I was diagnosed for a crime performed in the era of Reverend King and cover-up of a black civil rights leader whose values and morals tipped the charts in a continuous movement by his "I Have a Dream" and "On the Mountaintop" speeches. The Almighty weighed the altitude of racism, power, money, and the voices of millions in the United States of America at his death. I thought I was being monitored to die for the miracles that we knew but by the concept of sex was to the extreme. If you ask me, this was about the mystery of two million dollars.

I was in the world but not of the world. I had surrendered my life to Christ in 1984 in part as He raised me in His admonition of righteousness justified by His existence in His death, burial, and resurrection. This process shaped and molded my mind into the mind of Christ by His Word, prayer, praise, and worship as a new creature under the sovereignty of His will. I perceived the will of the Feds violated me as a free person. The Heavenly Father proved His love for the world and His people chosen to captivate the unbelievers by Christ Jesus (John 3:16).

In 1984, Reverend Jessie L. Jackson ran for the Democratic presidential candidacy. I had already alerted his campaign of the September 7, 1983, occurrence. In fact, he mentioned Dr. King "crying out from his grave" due to the US injustices in his national address at the Democratic Convention, which caught my attention and no one else's. People I talked to said they "don't remember."

My knowledge of using taxpayers' monies under Reagan grew to heights I could only imagine, seeing the daily discourse of spiritual warfare as an evil white man employed by life. I'll never know how many participants there were who staged being products of law enforcers with military knowledge in their background. I did not know the FBI was liable for miracles instead of the church and had to follow the cost from the Railroad. The psychiatrists put all their knowledge and treatment into a pill or injection regardless of the root cause of spirituality, hatred, racism, and money. But the average person outside the stressful arch of medication, Jesus, and the Body of Christ would have never succeeded in remaining psychologically sound enough to become a hired case manager.

The spirit has to be addressed like money matters to those who step into a control and conquer that build various other lifestyle claims of diverse ideations as the way to recovery. Money principles cannot flourish in contempt of life in its full season. There is vengeance in the Body of our Lord and Savior to refute the changes. I believed Jesus Christ was another reason for the Feds in devising this plan in the supernatural. Yet they had to subtract and attack to cover up two million dollars.

In my opinion, there are choices to be admonished as a leader in this covert operation that leads to the demise of a nation who prides itself on power and money. For the love of money is the root of all evil (1 Tim. 6:10). Reaganomics was a hefty two-time loser. This began the fall of the middle class of yesteryear. The economic recession as a world leader has declined to a low since 1929 and has embraced such a reflection by the market as the use of weaponry for mass fluctuation on Wall Street. No weapon formed against me shall prosper.

I thought the hit on Reverend King was to the detriment of the country since its creed of government involvement by the FBI and the "mystery of his money." For the power of a nation to rule by money and color changes the outcome of the degree of his influence by the affluent or the wicked in high places. The mental health of a person's value system developed as a bipartisan member of emancipation in the American way, which enforces the fancy of magistrates. Racism rears those ancestors who bend the minds of justice as a colony whitewashes and blacklists their own to an American resolution, which vilifies the fate of its economy because of influence, color, and greed.

The Just One who loves justice openly acknowledged a small army of martyrs to suffice the transgressions and iniquities of this present age of the American government. The United States flag appeared and elevated to the crown of my head as I completed the crossword puzzle clue, which was slay. I answered kill. Immediately, the Star-Spangled Banner dropped onto the newspaper from the depths of my mind surrounded by a hideous sight in the background. Once again, I thought I had confirmation and experienced terrorist repercussions by the adversaries or the FBI that Dr. King identified. Heaven knows the violence taken by force (Matt. 11:12). Jesus cannot sit idly by while a foreign country takes their lives for the innocence of God's people who needed a holy war intervention.

It took approximately two months to come to my senses about the elect of the Body of Christ. I needed Jesus to open up my spiritual eyes to a new day and to keep my baseline at the highest level of my mental status. The torment and ridicule about the sanctity of the Body of Christ was separated temporarily.

Trevor relieved some of the stress by his presence. "Upon this rock, I will build my church, and the gates of hell will not prevail against it" (Matt. 16:18). The warfare of my Lord and Savior rests its case of joy unspeakable to consecrate my hope in God although I was in an unrighteous condition. The steadfastness and perseverance of prayer rebuked the white serpent from putting me into an everlasting darkness of war. In a pit of hell for twenty to thirty years stressed its accomplishments of victimization and nothingness. It was all lies.

The undying love and appreciation Christ gave me to develop into a victory as an overcomer instead of as a victim was overwhelming. One who wept on several occasions inwardly and outwardly due to the despair of wickedness by the government or the Antichrist with seemingly never-ending demonic strongholds on my body and in the left hemisphere of my brain resulted in affecting my mind. It was a mountain to climb all the way up on this Christian journey. The ebb flowed to outrageous heights as venomous spiritual bodies always engulfed my head at its lowest point. Time conditioned me to stronger characteristics of Christ by a gracious leader as God Almighty in the midst of heavenly hosts. The "battlefield of the mind," as Joyce Meyer said, rested not in the laurels of humanity but in the God I serve.

Computer technology has made stammer, confused, and perplexed the mind of mankind for lack of safety by dangerous maneuvers on my brain. Its use by enemy design harbored procedures and statements of doom into memories of resentment. No machine can ever replace the source of energy and the will of the Holy Spirit that abided within the saints of God. My human rights deflected the occult as the fight receptor according to society and embraced Jesus's battle program from my faith versus a computer chip.

Satan could not be more contemptible by his intentions to mask the hidden plot into utter chaos and success of terrorizing me as a thing. I stood in the living room of my heart and slowly acknowledged the work of the Lord. I patiently endured amid a riot of woes by attacks from Jesus's archenemy. My faith abounded from knowing from the beginning that our victory would prevail in this war.

Dr. King, in his infinite state of spirit and soul, continued to guide my footsteps to Christ. I believed the law enforcement agency schemed to emulate the death of MLK Jr. in my mind for civil rights and refused me the right to live on purpose in the will of God the Father. As a discharged angel, he meant for me to caution my spirit of want for retribution. Vengeance is mine. I shall repay, saith the Lord.

As a disciple of Jesus in the twenty-first century, I learned to write the illumination of the darkness of my schizophrenic sentence on paper. I am not faulting my allegiance to this Holy War. But torment has no sorrow that heaven cannot heal. God won the war single-handedly against the territorial savage beasts of the American flag enraged by His finger of love for me. This unholy war cannot compute my frustrating degrees of intolerance aggravated by time standing still, amid orders to give it his best shot by whatever means necessary in the occult.

As the years lapsed, things were apparently getting worse. I tried not to lose sight of victory. I believed the plane with the Fed leader in it did a lot of witchcraft by positioning his men and females strategically so they could live comfortably despite the sorcery. While under their iron fists, I gripped and grappled accusations of allegations of being a traitor. Contempt for my life by thought transference and supernaturally in my central intelligence took a toll upon my nervous system. Their mission statement of "F—— you, motherf——r!" accompanied with a shot into heaven as they sealed the expletives in a curl of wind like a trapdoor. Jesus showed me He dodged the bullet while sitting on His throne.

I planned to get a CAT scan at Bellevue Hospital in New York because I complained of severe headaches. It was around Easter time. As I walked to the subway station from the medical center following the procedure, I felt a wall of wood spike from the base of my brain. I felt for sure the CAT scan revealed the US flag and sorcery that was hidden. The Lord avenged their diabolical scheme by the threat of terrorism we live in and the instability of the economy. But nonbelievers are the number one barrier to the truth (whether anyone wants to accept it or not). My CAT scan was" normal," whatever that meant, to objects and foreign bodies I knew were lodged in my brain. I deduced the falsifying labeling as a schizophrenic that plagued my existence of being punished for their government crimes and conspiracy.

In Christianity, God renews the mind because it is subject to change. He regulates it as part of His salvation plan of regeneration, sanctification, and glorification processes. Old habits, which were detrimental to the Body of Christ, were forgiven and forgotten by the death, burial and resurrection of Jesus Christ through the justification process.

Dr. King's demise should explain my stance of allegiance since he is an influential leader, a "drum major for justice," "a man of the cloth," a civil rights pioneer, and a fallen hero of African descent. He is an encourager of Christianity who practiced his faith. As a forerunner of the 1964 civil rights act, he retaliated against Klansmen in their black and white affairs by being nonviolent.

The Bible says that heaps of coal will fall upon their head (Prov. 25:22). I thought the FBI gung ho attitude of delusional points of hypocrisy about me and what I stand for as the Body of Christ wanted me to misrepresent the Christian community of blood-washed believers. Although I had gone astray, I was still a child of God, a work in progress. I felt I needed Trevor. Mind- boggling witness awed by the lessons of mass confusion pointed to misinterpretation and misrepresentation in His ministry.

God knows the heart. This is not about me. The enemy has eluded themselves into extinct visions of monstrosities beyond the centuries and the following of Satan despising the salvation plan. I glorified God. The Antichrist of my mind tarried between the solemn state of Dr. King and a usual fun-filled day of fools. Folly numbed me beyond the challenges and tested King Jesus by the violence of sorcery as a satanic playground in my head.

The way of overwhelming fly-by-night work by foolish unbelievers inspired the gall of a state of seclusion and melancholy as a chronic but temporary way of life. I believed increasing the depths of agony, depression, and mental anguish perplexed the mind into a chemical imbalance, and was a high price to pay for the government organization cash flow to spend frivolously as the plot thickened. Nevertheless, vital aspects of being tallied in a world of illusions by the black arts emitted by proven points of the occult stole from my existence in a typical day of terrorism. My mind among their insensitive, consuming, wanton spoken words of profanity prayed to override their insanities, which cause death.

Life was being taken from me daily. Regardless of my prayers and matters of the heart, which persisted to be extremely cautious in powers of darkness by violent days of danger and distress amid bloodthirsty contentment of veins saturated while hot blood from animals of a higher order became criminally insane, lawlessness tarried in a way to bind the captive, and normlessness inspired the belief of Holy Ghost-filled grievance for me. The treason degree by lack of patriotism has encumbered a sense of walk by faith complementary to the promises (2

Cor. 5:7) of protection-, joy-, and peace-filled days of abundant living and a life righteous of God blinding me with the Dr. King memory as overseer. In my innocence of prayer, I was prepared for this long walk.

Hatred abounds on a never-ending daily basis amid destruction of the mentality of the innocent mind construct. Looming methods of terrorism in the body continued to awe me, so the aggravation and agony is doubly heartfelt. I thought the aggravation of the assault band played on me by the judgment of the FBI was sickening with profanity. I beware of the tactics expressed in full length of my day fighting the good fight of faith defeating the foe into a frenzy of dissension and ill will.

"Be still and know that I am God: I will be exalted among the heathen. I will be exalted in the Earth" (Ps. 46:10). I'm just saying the Feds' constant morale of hate-filled stir-crazy expletives of tempered grief and sorrow affected the mind-set as depression set in. The sounds of retaliation are trumpets called to duty for the archangel Michael, who reverberated within my soul. I gave thanks to God for His vigilance in this matter of deadly forgery of a mechanism, sex, marriage, and power issues due to the color of my skin and money. My prayers were translated from profanity, which was a deterrent for me. But I had to pray in order to keep my sanity. Any claims of torture to the maximum degree and concentration on strongholds far beyond the intense torment of their evil spirituality by inflicted pain kept them satisfied.

As a contrary order by a broken back of mental health relief meant institutionalization was inevitable because of my imagination. My beliefs were overpowering and my faith extremely high. This artificial schizophrenia was excruciating, and the telltale signs of sorcery beside the tempestuous microorganisms of hate, doubt, gall, and the belief of killing me, whispering under any other circumstances of death-gratifying feats, would have prevailed.

But defying their mission statement of witchcraft and a curse was an employable session for therapeutic solutions among the doctors of recovery. Chilling proportions of hate eerily never checked themselves for higher grounds of mercy views by the need for grace under increased death threats. Words of strife affected the norm into a fanfare of lies, self-righteousness and terrorism besides the lawlessness and normlessness of the supernatural.

I believed beleaguering cursed the land of the USA due to failures by the principality fight of an embarrassing end of stealing the very air I breathe into gasps of victorious loss. The spiritual legality to assault me whenever a sexual encounter was engaged hid behind their wedding bands and our fornication through panic attacks. Every sexual action was designed to kill me by their words, which carried powers of darkness from the black arts or the occult. Trevor had to go.

In 2007 and 2008, the economy of social justice surfaced along the path as sophisticated keepsakes, as the almighty dollar amounted to near bankruptcy on Wall Street due to corruption and misappropriation of funds. The deficit escalated, teemed, and abounded as the dead presidents scaled recession tread upon ludicrous developments upon my mind of war. Though in jeopardy, the market of greed gave safety nets and risked insufficiencies in accommodating their claims of setbacks by brinks of a complete downward spiral.

I believed the US economic state of mind was on the verge of another recession due to deceptive and blatant disdain for the right to live. So the banks, Wall Street, the auto industry, and the housing markets took the hit. As Ward of the State, sometimes my God administered financial wounds due to the embarrassing realization of possible blood money, which initiated Democratic concepts of life into the toilet of refuse.

Over eighteen trillion in debt speaks for itself. Violence was all they cared to understand. Terrorism and racism took on a whole new meaning of eerie and gut-wrenching horrific tactics because they too risked judgement in the private sector of this suicide because of finances. I believed the FBI has jumped off the financial cliff into the recession of hatred. A holy war was necessary. Signs of white-collar crimes cluttered my mind cautiously with their high-positioned design of thievery and terrorism. Peace will escalate never again in this lifetime without realizing in this world there is a God to glorify. Taunts unmask hoods by the blood and finances of Dr. King expressed by protests in the watch of Obama.

I believed from the very onset of this great FBI blunder that the G-men Freudian slip and guilt complex of being "a rat, a thief, and a killer" fed on the human countenance of my peace as they encircled me. Due to the orders from animal-like instincts, repulsive invested attacks to contend with the Almighty through me with wickedness and fury in law enforcement was ruthless. I am an African American and a disciple of Dr. Martin Luther King Jr., who, in the interim, became my spiritual father.

I protested by following the National Action Network under the leadership of Reverend Al Sharpton on occasions. I brought my white gloves and returned to service as gatekeeper for the Lord by peaceful protests of a few firefighters and the advertising organizations we had issues with as African American people. I attended a number of rallies in the village of Harlem and stayed abreast of their work by radio.

In my opinion, the Federal Bureau of Investigation assimilated within society as one of the most revered subculture of the US government, exhibiting loss of judgment with morals of cannibals who at times possessed a conscience when I instigated. Protected and guided by their female counterpart who follows a commander from a vein of dedication, loyalty, and speech by a male chauvinist regardless of the final destination, it was defiant. I thought the leader liberally gave orders from a lifetime commitment of service to eternal damnation by a demented mind. I believed a lifestyle of disobedience by his admissions of FBI operations and maneuvers by contract controlled their behavior. In my opinion, they employed crafty killer instincts haphazardly to squelch my Christian-faith principles. They wore body armor strategically upon their chest as the sounds of guns fired command and commented feverishly to conceal the guilty ill-fated bent minds of war.

They fight me, and I fight them in a good fight of Christian Word and prayer. I won the battle of innocence by being a black, proud, and contented Christian woman holding up the bloodstained banner. I deduced the federal body of warmongering upon foreign lands such as Iraq, heavenly angels, and Jesus subjugated, and guided me from the depths of conflict representing the Almighty God. The triggers of life, like secret matters of the King assassination in an offensive foul play of righteousness, led to insanity. I believed their tyranny surrounded and penetrated the complete left hemisphere of the brain's normal functioning.

I was framed by this conspiracy of attempted murder, terrorism, and schizophrenia. They tried to start maneuvers on the right as they worked constantly on my memory. Their supernatural artificial symptoms pressed upon my sternum, occipital lobe, inner ear, and spinal cord, which activated unknown evil talents by recall of a diabolical rehearsal customized to hear their approach. A wise human cannot phantom their communist ideals in my left hemisphere of the brain, which dominated my rights beyond computerized and mechanical fear of the occult. Success to withstand the spiritual confusion of messaging failures, expletives, and assault as a thing was often wondered. What kind of an administration paid for this type of Antichrist or false profit?

Usually, I weigh approximately 200 pounds. After fasting and praying, I reached 126 pounds three times successfully during thirty years of combat. Prayer without ceasing (1 Thess. 5:17) was my refuge and shield of sanctity of sanity. I complained and murmured to Jesus nonstop about the implications of being insane. Fasting was something I mostly heeded because of the unknown of going through a time of hardship. I had to go through due to my long supplication of prayer at the Railroad. It was necessary to turn over my plate so the Lord could work with my man-made schizophrenia and the imagination of torment that made me act out. After being diagnosed with paranoid schizophrenia, I always kept what I going through to myself until it started to manifest in my daily living. I did not want to be judged by someone's ignorance of spiritual warfare.

At future employments, I stayed anonymous due to its nature and the healthy mind-set in society as noticeable traits of lowly meekness and mildness, as a Christian demeanor prevailed. But I had the tendency for my disease to sneak the pressure build up on me. I needed medication for the stress of leading a double life. I talked about God and the injustices of this world. I was always high functioning without the meds for the most part. Overcome with the burdens of spiritual insanity of rhetoric in my life while on spiritual assignment, I studied and learned the ramifications of the King assassination.

This spiritual journey indoctrinated by prayer, faith, grace, mercy, justice, the old biblical "law," and the Word of God as the norm guaranteed a win.

I graduated summa cum laude in undergrad and studied the Bible sporadically within thirty years until I learned to read it every day. As I read the Bible, the enemy would add and subtract words that voided the Word and had serious consequences (Rev. 22:18-19). I write from my own experience rather than the saints of God's findings on powers of darkness, or "we wrestle not against flesh and blood" (Eph. 6:12). I might beg to differ. We can be possessed or occupied by the supernatural. None of the pastors whom I sat under wanted to deal with spiritual warfare. They knew it meant crazy and demons.

I could not use a carnal weapon (not that I wanted to) but the sword of the tongue in the words of Christ (2 Cor. 10:4). I believed I had a punch that would break my fist. Yet their stiff neck attitudes derived a new beginning to battle the Almighty with satanic decisions to crawl, beg, borrow, and steal my thoughts to arrest my talking to God on a continuing basis. They inquired of His plans to control the psychological state of war by answered prayers. Their wicked course of action was foolishness, alluring no one to fight in expletives.

However, the criminal acts started as their fight of what they continued was irreversible. Jesus Christ in a dying world of massive casualties and despair of terrorism embattled their own self-hatred as a lost and losing faction. I believed my foe plagued the land of opportunity with various temptations of deaths and economic loss. As enemy of the state and for the love of an angel, who meant this country of Christian beliefs of martyrdom was incredibly acclaimed but not by my choice. Dr. King and his predecessors as targets of the KKK Unionists hold these truths to be self-evident. According to the Constitution, that belonged to so many who believed in their quest to end personal and political grave sites of those who made their mark on this world for change.

I prayed that Dr. King did not die in vain due to a select few of camp-style riders. I believed the guilt of this organization, the FBI, declined to see the error of its ways in the sixties, except to see it fit to cuss his eulogy and the meaning of his character yet in the eighties. I deduced they sought my life because I had the power, knowledge as an advocate for Christianity and the legacy question of Dr. King's two million dollars.

As a man of the cloth, first and foremost, he could never have lied in his eternal state. It was a clue, a mystery to solve. It was not of his character as a mortal to lie. Jesus had to tell him what to say. This supernatural act can be misinterpreted by the saints of God by deceiving his meaning and changing the outcome. The civil liberty of a fellow saint or brother in Christ Jesus intercepted the life of a woman who followed the teachings of Jehovah, which means the truth to "we the people" of the Christian faith.

I believed the year of a democratic farce as a citizen in the forefathers' principles have become null and void, but reign from everlasting to everlasting regardless of fools will always stand. Portrayal of a mockery of the Bible for freedom and equality uphold the justice of foundations to have a godly stance. It relegates the love for this country of liberalism and humanitarian feats of Christianity as based upon His Word.

I believed I was young and strong in the faith to suffer persecution in my life with an unjust national power with Army affiliates or ties. Jesus worked in mysterious ways and has used His servants to send a message to America. The enemy taught me to kill or be killed, obviously, to survive a war. I have been branded with a diagnosis by the courts of a serious mental illness of schizophrenia, a lifetime sentence. It's a sentence whereas a diagnosis of religiously preoccupied is a losing battle and perceived to be a barrier for mental health recovery. It was a war of words and action that carried a death sentence.

Nevertheless, Jesus is a Deliverer, Healer, Way Maker, and Mind Regulator in whom I believe trust and obey rather than the course of study as a fear monger of psychiatry. He specialized in working with the mind and the heart. By the Word of God and by his stripes, I am healed (Isa. 53:5). The mental health issues were due to systemic ignorance of laymen in its field of psychiatry by the exclusion of the spirit and its claim of medicine as being humane. They know that man has a spirit but dare not address it in psychology. I have a spiritual problem that chemical imbalances are justified by the faith experts to diagnose.

Man has been battling mental illness before psychiatry was discovered. Jesus often cast out demons in His life on earth, in the Gospel of the New Testament. Regardless, some still would rather believe in evolution and the big bang theory, whereas I cared to believe in the Holy Bible (Genesis). As a discomfort to my soul, which consists of the emotions, the will and the mind with medications at disproportionate levels have serious side effects. Psychotropic medications not only treated the chemical imbalance but also affected the normal balance of chemistry in the body, causing side effects like delusional thoughts.

I don't believe in all the glory of modern medicine and science. They alleviated the stress and give you symptoms, which get worse. I regretted waking up in a secluded environment of locked doors with keys to a cage. I still had the occult spiritual problem. A natural diet with proteins and supplements maintained a restful, peaceful demeanor by the grace of God. "It is written. Man shall not live by bread alone but, by every word that proceeded out of the mouth of God" (Matt. 4:4).

My faith recognized the world of medicine. But the Word of God, prayer, and fasting are also recognized by the clergy when it comes to mental health issues. A correlation of spirituality should be recognized by psychiatry because it does have its place. A nonbeliever should be handled accordingly on a case- by-case basis. Choose this day who you will serve, mammon or the Most High Father, Son, and Holy Spirit. I fully understand I did not call on Brother Mohammed, Buddha, or Confucius because they died, just like Osama and Dr. King. They all were spirit-led prophets back in their day, but I needed remission of sins and to turn over my plate. I needed peace of mind, miracles, forgiveness, and power. By His Grace, I live believing because of the Son.

Anabel, the negro girl, has to have the last word. She is a mutant above and beyond the black race that has ever produced legitimately as an enemy of incarnate mind in her criminal insanities. A fight ensued, and she was slapped with a fine money could not pay. She led the white man into calling the Holy Spirit d———n sh———. There need not be an awesome replay in my mind. Hell's fury laughs and waits to grip her cursed tongue like rhetoric in the intangible web of torment. She hatched in 1985 from out of nowhere.

Picture her mistakenly within her demonic structure piercing the earhole of the supernatural and embracing her valor to creep as a thief. Stalking awaits me to open my eyes to white and black shoulders with venom burning their insides to win the war. Her folly is pathetic, rude, boisterous, and obnoxious.

This is no joke or laughing matter when we are talking about life. Her caricature does not soothe me. Under a rock she crawled out and refuses to return. I thought she has led the Feds in dangerous territories of a spiritual nature that the FBI now had to follow to the death. I heard her cuss the Holy Ghost, and the white man eagerly pursued her insanities against the Savior for free. That seed giver is capable of intentionally seeking her out as the most notorious, dumb, female subspecies on this side of heaven. In my opinion, she cursed and added to their low-life imagination in my plight. Every waking moment was filled with drama. She was also a Taurus the Bull—just some things Festus would look for to spite me. Undoubtedly, Festus discussed me with her.

The deception and unrest was blamed upon me by the Great Accusers for their paths to hell. Their satanic demonic unrighteous living germinated a Junior, a son with two biblical names (God with us) and a son from another man. They continued to blame me for their ungodly decisions in life and the irony of Festus marrying an Army soldier who had his female child also. This was for self-protection of his rights as an unaccountable head of household. He still remembers his account back in the password days of God because I complained about them voluntarily being in my spiritual hearing and side effects.

I thought the Feds' skywriting of Festus as the Messiah meant all prayers went to the spirit of Festus first. The Holy Spirit has been profaned by creatures of two hands and two feet. This was not a war game and never fun- filled folly for me. This was not just a war of words.

Their mission statement, I knew not at this time. This was my faith in God. I believed since he should have retired from his Fed job, I hope seeing it is over thirty years later, I was always better off without whatever I kept or discarded. I am for the most part freed by the Blood of the Lamb of being possessed.

Anabel and I never had a conversation. After thirty years, I fervently attempted to keep the monologue to a minimum. I dislike her with a passion. She was my archenemy, and the man in the plane was God's. Anabel was someone I learned about by her ruthless haunting. I believed Festus and the government prompted her to be the thorn in my side. I presumed she was especially chosen for this purpose. We are complete opposites, or so I heard from his family. The war waged against heaven and in her female flesh. I desired nothing from her for her soul and spirit to haunt. I could not physically see my attacker all the time, but every waking moment, she was there heckling in her animated role. I could not shake hallucinations of Anabel, and her spirit remains to be my Achilles heel of talk.

I tried to reason with her about the Lord and what He supposedly did to her. She failed immensely to prove He did anything but love her by shedding His blood and having mercy on her life. She always wanted to discuss my past failures to get rid of the thought of theirs. I just learned in 2013 how to turn her over to the Lord without picking her back up. I finally learned how to "let go and let God." All my attempts were futile, and I tried for years. I became adamant about washing my hands of her (Matt. 27:24). She never shuts up. I do not know all what I did to her through Festus. I thought it was a repercussion for sleeping around in Christianity. But I was remorseful, and told her. It still did not work.

"I'm just saying" I do not know how the Feds hooked her up to my left hemisphere. One day, she broke through the spiritual realm. She was not always there. His mother and brother informed me that she cusses like a sailor.

That last word seems like it would have never been realized. I finally gave it to her. I have never threatened her about anyone. I tried to talk to her when she was pregnant with her first. But she backed up in fear. I do not know what Anabel heard about me. But I definitely was not going to fight her, even if she was not pregnant. She had it all wrong, obviously. Even though the voices have subsided, I thought the FBI still whispers and follows her lead. I do not want anyone talking in my spiritual realm except God. I don't want the memories. So life would go on.

I was totally consumed by the Holy Ghost after a barrage of heavy haunting in the head and in the body. In the late nineties, I had felt worse. I was thinking about Jesus who suddenly made His appearance while I was fully clothed in my right mind. (I was always in my right mind while under attack.)

The assault was nonstop, except when Jesus presented Himself. My demeanor changed from a state of depression to instant euphoria. He was right in the midst of this ungodly war.

Spiritual warfare never again experienced this freedom of release in my physical state, and just as quick, he was gone. The Spirit of Christ consumed me from head to toe. But I was so debilitated. I ended up in the psych ward later that day. My imagination ran wild. I knew instead of being handcuffed they should have carried me out as royalty on a throne. I was King of kings and Lord of lords.

I pled for his rapture. The physical toll my heart suffered with the enemy was short of miraculous. I did not develop hypertension or have a heart attack. I could wholeheartedly pray for their soul salvation and mean them well. I tried to find terms to forgive and forget; however, neither was an option. I was diagnosed for a lifetime with schizophrenia. I was outnumbered daily as a byproduct of embarrassing ungodly truths. I believed the Feds were desperate, made up lies, and deceived themselves into believing their own intricate pattern webbed by saved computer chips and videotapes of rapture-like material ruin me.

People lied on Dr. King because they could find no fault in him (CNN). He was influential, loved by his wife, family, friends, community, and those who supported him. He loved mankind. On the other hand, when my lifestyle changed for the better, they would replay my guilt into deviant memories until the evil mastermind source of frenzy dominated my thought pattern again. I could hear Jesus swatting them in the spiritual realm. This was important to me. Just the thought of Dr. King overshadowed and undauntedly proved the way of salvation.

Jesus continued to reveal, correct and abolish the web of sick hatred, curses, profanity, gall, aggravation, brainwashing, the occult, sorcery, normlessness, and lawlessness in my life. The satanic spirits still resided within my head. The crime of tarrying in the human body, the human mind, the human spirit, and the human brain forfeited nothing less but torture. I thought they replayed events repeatedly in the powers of darkness for a full satanic effect.

The Holy Spirit knows I labored tirelessly in well doing. Yet I was not in His will. "God is not mocked" (Gal. 6:7), as the thought of Christ's imminent return encouraged me with words of wisdom, truth, and authority. The end of this world, as we knew it, was over. "If my people who are called by my name would humble themselves and pray, seek my face and turn from their wicked ways. Then will they hear from heaven and I will heal their land" (2 Chron. 7:14). It will never be the same due to the use of terrorism, a satanic strategy of profanity against God, His people, and the elect.

Now you have same sex marriage. I believed their integrity as the defeated foe was eradicated by their haste and waste of assault. How could a pill relieve and alleviate military grandeur when war in the skies was the limit and was lurking? They stripped me with their poignant signs of psychopathic deviant behaviors from a great distance in the sky and on land.

My people always pray for the president, for political and governmental decisions. However, this adversary of God has a boiling, breaking, and turning point of detestable social ills that are indescribable to people of a profound religious order. The electricity in the synapse of my nerves reflected a spirit of the flesh assured by a round of racial abomination. This world has fallen into deep waters of sorrow and determination by an electrical shock of despair and profanity. It has declined sharply by the economy into an atmospheric perilous pressure, like the years of havoc and turmoil since 1929.

I believed the war of words was unworthy of protective measures due to allowing accusations, intervention, indiscretions override and emergence of expletives plague the heavens war was protected, profaned and cursed. I perceived the KKK and its tyranny of communistic, self-righteous, or ungodly ventures uphold the labor force of the FBI as an excuse cover-up by two females and mainly two males. I have one sarcastic induced symptom, and it has nothing to do with the meds administered. It is Anabel as a spirit. This war was profaned and cursed.

I worked at Franklin Men's Shelter in the Bronx in 1986 as a caseworker before leaving to relocate to Georgia. The daily stress of the government working in my head led to memories in my environment of hardship. I divulged my Dr. King secrets to those whom I drew close to as an employee with an unknown diagnosis. In August 1989, I began to work for the Child Welfare Administration. My employment lasted for nine years before resigning due to disability and family pressures to resign.

I was still a member of the community church, nondenomination with a Baptist-leading discipleship. The minister, soon to become reverend, took an interest in my case and prayed for me. He has visited me in the hospital, and his support was much appreciated. In over thirty years of being diagnosed, the minister was the only shepherd who visited the sick and shut in. The old pastor cringed as I hugged him for lack of a familiar face from the Christian community. I shall never forget his being turned off.

The minister had a kinder, gentler, more compassionate approach. The old pastor supposedly taught love to his congregation, but I beg to differ. I never at this time was so humiliated by a man of the clergy as my pastor. He did not offer to pray with me, seeing the situation on the eleventh floor at Elmhurst Hospital. I was hospitalized by the staff for at least six weeks, which was always excessive before threats of Creedmoor circulated in my hearing. I probably would have become suicidal had this mental institution become one of my hospitalizations.

I was never violent but was coded "blue" for mouthing off at the head nurse. Consequently, I reported two nurses for apathetic and elated treatment while a patient was in distress. I observed to protect others and preserved myself from staff after viewing codes. The charge nurse and her coworker were overly stimulated in a state of excitement and euphoria before restraints. Everyone is at risk at these times, and there was never a happy moment. I wrote to the Office of Mental Health with my complaint. They also contacted me in reference to Dr. King. So did the National Action Network. However, I did not know how they could have helped me at the time. I acknowledged and thanked them, anyway. I know the nurses could not wait until it was my turn. I acquired a big mouth at the wrong time in life. I had to learn to speak up in order to protect myself, and I am still learning from Kings County Hospital or future employment.

I managed to enroll my child as an intern at Harvard University at the age of sixteen and boarding school, at the Tabor Academy of Marion, Massachusetts. At my request, Jesus kept her in his watchful eye when I felt ostracized by society due to overactive artificially induced symptoms and imagination. He was her guardian, and by His grace, I also managed to put her through undergrad at Connecticut College. She resents me for "raising herself," she said.

SPIRITUAL WARFARE AT ITS BEST

worked at Franklin Men's Shelter, I eventually relocated to the Atlanta, Georgia, area in 2000 for clues, follow- up, and aid from anyone willing or close to the King family to assist in any way they saw fit in my life. I thought I needed insight—perhaps revelation or knowledge may be an encouraging word—but I didn't want to trouble anyone about the Federal Bureau of Investigation. I would often go to the Southern Christian Leadership Conference (SCLC), the King Center, and Dr. King' s crypt for solace amid a dangerous unhealthy mission due to what I believed to be government activity in Queensbridge.

I reached out to SCLC regularly but never got a response. I did not know how to write my plight down on paper. I wrote down the insanities that kept popping into my mind, may they be satanic or the Resh. To my amazement, the war was just as intense in the South as in the North. The assault ended in 2001. My demeanor was serene as I frequented the King burial site on the grounds of the old Ebenezer Baptist Church. Nevertheless, time went on, and the war never subsided markedly due to the inner battlefield of this mind-set. It was on Vine Street I received a closer walk with God the Father. I was able to buy a 1998 Saturn vehicle with my city pension and employment at the Jennie A. Clarke Family Shelter in Manhattan.

Any signs of discovery were always subject to something dangerous and new. I believed the FBI's fear emanated from hatred for the Holy Trinity or Godhead as well. I had repented for all my sins for the most part under the law of the Father that no longer applied under His infinite wisdom of a new covenant with His people and His redemptive story of Grace through Jesus Christ. I had nothing to feel guilty about, but Satan is the great accuser by his wiles of confusion, and distractions from the past thirty to forty years weighed heavily on my mind. My own imagination would get me hospitalized. My daughter says I talk about God a lot when I am sick. I believe and know there is a God whereas "all things are possible" (Matt. 19:26).

Elmhurst Hospital would overdose me with pure lithium as it physically pulled my mind out of shape, like Turkish taffy. I was mustering all my faith to set the captives free and started to act out with a big chest with big muscles. Lithium was used for egocentric problems. I passed out. They never prescribed that again, although I was prescribed with lithium bicarbonates. People in general take advantage and misconstrue the mentally ill regardless of their intent in life. I was sexually seduced by an orderly and sexually molested by a gynecologist during an internal examination. The Chinese doctor knew I took medication because it was written in my chart. That is why he knew he could have his way with me. I felt helpless.

While in solitary confinement, I usually slept off the injection and regretted missing my mom and aunt, who visited me nearly every day. I believed my government troubles had an effect on my mental state even after being medicated. The spiritual realm vied for my attention regardless of my environment and consumption of meds. I was at risk of being overdosed or zonked out. I no longer wanted to get high. God was the only answer that didn't require pills and needles to solve my problems. I always required a low dosage. I just needed something in my system to cope with the physical pain, which brought about the delusional thoughts.

In 2000, Atlanta was when I called upon the Lord to cease the enemy from troubling, and anyway, He saw it fit to bless me. I rested in knowing that trouble does not last always. I knew Reverend King was a man of God who would assist watching over me and would like to protect me from myself. But his eternal sleep comes first, and his labor was not in vain. I am saved, sanctified, and full of the Holy Ghost.

The King family released a book of sermons entitled "A Knock at Midnight." I felt sure they received my account of September 7, 1983. His wife, Coretta Scott King, held a book signing at the King Center auditorium. I requested she write the date and sign her name. But she refused. She wanted me to write it. It would have been more meaningful if she wrote it for me. I did not want to trouble her or her family. I could see and hear that the civil rights movement had affected her and that was not the time to argue or explain. We were about to make a scene. I wrote her family in 1986. The death of her beloved husband struck a hostile chord. I already had insisted without too much information. The book was eventually stolen in Gwinnett County.

Anyway, her husband made me feel significant, proud, empowered, and encouraged to run this race unto the end. I am determined to live to see what the end is going to be. His book of sermons was advanced as well as inspirational. I had never heard sermons with such insight, caliber, and knowledge of the material before him. I was so fascinated and intrigued by this Baptist preacher and his teachings. I never heard it before in the Baptist Church. Now that I am a seasoned saint, I would love to have the book.

I made arrangements to reside with a girlfriend in Douglasville, Georgia, in 2000. I secured employment working for the Department of Family and Children Services (DFACS) for two weeks. I assessed the thoughts of motherhood or parenting of the children and took my job extra seriously. I was working on only criminal cases that were already adjudicated by the courts. My job was to contact and update the closed cases. I dealt with the law and criminal minds of the parents or legal guardians.

I began to analyze the criminal mind and their wicked actions. The weight of DFACS and the KKK extremely absorbed my judgment and insight that stated clearly needed to open the cases that were at risk. I had to grow out of these types of dilemmas because I felt most of the cases, if not all, needed to be monitored. I recognized the transparency by the judicial system that indoctrinated them all with lessons about nurturing life. I was burned out, stressed, and mentally tired. My view was distorted and skewed by the parents who needed extra help.

I wanted to become a foster mom, and eventually adopt a sick child. I brought her to church with me and was not authorized. My mind told me that this black child was in the hands of a Klansman. I wanted to protect her from the signs of neglect by the foster parent.

I watched and prayed for twenty years that this torture would figure reprehensible to God while He overtly constrained their evil position, as animated behavior and as tenacious combatants continued to wage war upon my existence soared. I believed I toiled and tested government authorization simply due to unsolvable paths of justice. The point of living beyond the grave and white-supremacy theory conclusive to danger in a scheme pleasurable to slave trade mentality only concentrated on their poor judgment in Jesus's world.

I believed the killers of inalienable rights by government standards authorized tribunal strengths into a frenzy of fury and revenge of pure hatred. Convoluted smells of testiness converge on my olfactory glands because I admired a sweet-smelling savor, like Jesus. I heard them say this killer instinctual pattern risked in life as contrast related to the holding of their nose to powerful odors of secrecy by injustices. In my opinion, their deadly like instincts concluded in fallout toward their heroic stand of war against me were artificial and willful. I believed they achieved making their own killer instinct as mutually exclusive with the odors from feces and words. I did not see them holding their noses. You can easily detect the nasal difference. I never held my nose on cue. It had no meaning at that time. My instincts had to be accounted for, and killer was the last.

I began to frequent the Southern Christian Leadership Conference founded by Dr. King, a group that his son presided over with some difficulty. I wanted to meet with him for comfort, so I continued to correspond. I was also looking for a soul mate and did not know his present wife was his best friend. I felt there was a marriage made in heaven for me too. God is not a respecter of persons (Rom. 2:11), and I thought possibly one of his sons took on this trait.

Now, my deathbed request has changed. I made an appointment to see him, but he never acknowledged. I thought maybe his son could break the curse of the government or perhaps one of these black leaders who knew Dr. King personally could do something. Above all, I knew I had their prayers since they were basically men of the cloth.

In 2001, I went to Washington, DC, to introduce myself to whoever would listen, or perhaps to the president. I thought coming over the rolling hills of the Great Lawn were tranquil strides of destiny. I witnessed and gave honor to the Almighty God who watched the outcome of a long journey. Thrills of victory blared through my '98 Saturn to civilize the cup of wrath by Father God who earnestly gave his consent to speak my peace.

In the wee hours of the darkest mornings, I waited patiently to bestow upon a friend my plight as a disciple of Dr. King and of Jesus. A uniformed policeman approached me in the middle of my presentation meant for the civilians. After my freedom of speech, my concern was for my child a government mishap, which I intended to halt once and for all. During the Bush administration, my child gave way to a rebellious spirit toward me, an action that was perceived to be a major maturation issue. My immediate family had finally taken its toll on her. I would have stopped this world for my daughter and knocked on the president's door if they would let me. This epic saga began to hit home, and I was hurt.

My misery continued to come from Vine Street in Atlanta, where the Father led this incredible jaunt to the beginning of my sunrise to sunset. In His kingdom, I had started to develop a relationship and a newfound love for Father God. He blessed me on controversial matters, which I reviewed as acclaimed internationally in current events. He intellectually massaged and fed my mind. That was when my change was feeling strange and felt like foreign- currency counterfeit, or light.

I travelled around the Washington, DC vicinity looking for the proposed King monument site. As soon as I crossed the outskirt banks of the Potomac, I saw there was a street named in his honor. It was the slums of Washington. From an environment of colossal grandeur to a run-down poor neighborhood, I sighed with amazement. Dr. King's people were victimized far too long and looked poorer than public aid. Everything appeared to be trashed, worn, and dirty in this desolate area.

I rode around Washington, DC, and was harassed by the cops. I explained to the officer that I was sightseeing and kind of lost down the street from the Capital low-lying avenues. I guess my gospel music was a bit too loud, and I typically love loud music. On the other hand, it was my third time in the area within minutes, and I guess I became suspect for loud music.

I experienced some racism at the hotel where I was sleeping in my car. Several days passed before they caught on to my using their plush bathroom facilities. The last day, I was shown to a bathroom where they excreted their feces. It was not a grand hotel, after all. Again, I was so humiliated by white folk. Everything was black and white in the South in those days.

I attended Christian ministries in Georgia and was regarded as too radical for Christ. I hung on every word the pastor preached as he referred to the house of God as a hospital for the sick. I brought the foster child to see the clergy for prayer. Somehow, I believe I kept interfering with Pastor's Sunday- morning television broadcast. During the Sunday-morning service, they would ask me to leave the sanctuary and finally told me that I was no longer welcome. I paid my tithes and offering there whereby his wife or the pastor could have said something by pulling my coattail if I was too loud or offensive to anyone. They had even threatened to call the police when I was approached by an off-duty corrections officer. He had Rashed his badge and stated he was security. I responded, "So! What that mean to me on a Sunday morning in church?"

Sister Mary often told me that the Holy Spirit said to "stick with her." She left their ministry soon after I did because her worship was disturbed. Security would eject me from the house of prayer. Sister Mary came with me while they persecuted this child of God. I stood up for my rights but was still threatened.

All the churches in Georgia, I decided I could go someplace else. It was just I could not understand security at church. That is a bit too much for me. They restricted my praise and worship because it was a small church, and I guess I was too loud. I am an old-school Christian, and more conservative than I thought.

Sister Mary began to teach me my spiritual-warfare scriptures and led Bible study in her home. She was a devout Christian woman who walks upright before the Lord and keeps me lifted up in prayer before Jesus every day. She is an accomplished prayer warrior. As intercessor, she prays the prayers of the righteous to God and adapts the prayer to fit the problem. She wisely chooses the scriptures from the Bible as a sophisticated, well-versed woman of God. She has the gift of speaking in "other tongues" and listens attentively for a response. Otherwise, she does not make a move. We will always be sisters in Christ, and today she is my best friend in and out of the ministry.

The enemy was clever to camouflage his pathetic craft under the guise of suffering with schizophrenia. After being hospitalized for debilitating circumstances and twenty years of assault nonstop, the fight to keep my sanity worsened. If I never talked about it, you would never know I was at war. I had a lifetime sentence and suffered with a number of diagnoses, such as bipolar, manic depressive, religiously preoccupied, schizophrenia affective, paranoid type but basically psychotic. It was psychotic, according to science, and serious. I know what I experienced in over thirty years of being diagnosed. I should have never recovered from the insanity of cunning, subtle, hostile, rigorous, belligerent words from law enforcement tactics and profanity. The conspiracy of psychotic episodes and the illusive serious mental disorder haunted the existence of my child, family, and friends. I thought they might not understand the ramifications of what my role is amid the corrupt law enforcement with a military background. But I am now a key player with questions. I believed their deeds were to distract me and not question anymore about the two million dollars.

Secret errors of war occurred before, but I was given power nobody ever knew. A veteran account of the Vietnam War indicated the US Army of challenging events was swept under the rug as a dishonorable discharge with blunders. From what I understood from this soldier, a handful of families ran this country, something he dared not elaborate further out of fear. Honestly speaking, I would believe anything about the American government and what they call justice right about now.

Since terrorism effects and affects the American way and belief system of being the most powerful, their credit is failing in this world due to suicide bombers and terrorists.

I left Gwinnett County, Georgia, early in April 2001 to visit the St. Lorraine Hotel, where the assassination of Dr. King occurred. I was very brazen and I thought determined in my pursuit of reaching the world-renowned destination in Memphis, Tennessee. I did not have a battle or backup plan. I travelled on Route 85 South while traversing through Alabama, Mississippi, and Tennessee.

I reached Tuskegee University to and fro my trip south. Close to midnight, the remains of a ghost town left me in awe at the site where huge bells tolled every hour. Its eerie environment was awesome, as detectives stopped my curiosity near their railroad tracks. The Mississippi trenches in its rural habitat did not stop me from surveying the woods behind the farms in vast fields. I had discovered an adventurous streak in my complex personality makeup. I did not attribute this to schizophrenia, nevertheless dangerous.

I noticed the pills, over time, really worked in my nervous system and worsened it also. I rode planks across a pit, which seemed like miles in the fields because turning back was not a viable option. It was increasingly perilous due to a necessary wheel alignment on my vehicle, which warranted extreme caution. Respectfully, turning back was safest, but God was with me.

Finally, after much travel in the woods, I taught myself under divine watch how to turn left whenever I was in doubt. A left turn would lead to a main street from anywhere. I discovered this phenomenon really worked for me. I drove aimlessly in the hot sun to a destination of adventure. It was an amusement park. I did drive through tree-lined residential areas in Alabama and Tennessee without a GPS. But oftentimes, secluded areas where veer railways carried freight and people, scarcely populated the vicinity. Needless to say, I did not make it to the St. Lorraine. I was tired of driving and had a long ride home. I kept driving in the area of the roller coaster and government plant. It was too late, anyway. I needed some sleep and had not planned for a trip overnight.

Exhausted, I raced back to Georgia. I pulled off Route 85 North. The Lord informed me to "slow down." I somewhat obliged. On this residential street is where He asked me to do Him a favor. I thought about it and granted the request. I reflected upon all the things He had done for me. Jesus, in his own way, stated, "Whatever you do, don't stop." He repeated the request: "Don't stop." I had Jesus on my mind again.

As soon as I agreed, there came a fleet of police from Clayton County, Georgia. They had bright lights flashing and sirens blaring. I asked the Lord, "What should I do, because the sheriffs demanded that I pull over?" The pressure rose to an unhealthy level. So I pulled over. I faced train tracks to my left and law enforcement officers to my right. I was surrounded and flanked to pull off again.

I wore my Fred Hammond T-shirt, had my Bible in the passenger seat, and had the Good News of Jesus Christ playing in the background. The police pursued me under my control of speed. Mind you, in Alabama, it was Ku Klux Klan night. They asked me twice to wind down the window. I refused to wind it down. A colored police officer ended up smashing it. The sergeant pulled me out of the vehicle and "steered" me to the pavement like a cow or an animal.

They kept me like a common criminal. I was never arrested for obstruction of an officer and obstruction of procedure by the female Officer. The female officer never read me my Miranda rights. They told me three months later what I was arrested for at Georgia Regional—a mental institution.

I tried gospel music to set the captives free, like what Paul and Silas did. I finished in Clayton County Orientation of jail for three months before being incarcerated in the psych ward of Georgia Regional. I never called my family. Someone contacted them because I had no intentions. The harness of transport to the state facility was as if I was a killer. Transport was demeaning, degrading, and most humbling on the inside. I am proud to say, however, that I failed as a criminal because General Population was too taxing on my physical countenance and mind of Christ.

The unrest in Orientation triggered a lapse of time fit for a common criminal with nothing to live for and nothing promising in the immediate future. Basically, most of those whom I talked to were incarcerated and jailed for petty larceny. Sometimes there was a serious encounter, which led to a special task force to sweep the cells and inspect us. Violence occurred even with a plastic spork (spoon, fork), I guess.

I never learned about commissary procedure, and left fifty dollars untouched even though I needed things. Nobody explained about the complicated timed event, and I felt a big hassle. My brother visited me from Charlotte, North Carolina, on my birthday and left the money. He was the only one who would cry for me whenever he saw I was institutionalized. It affected my daughter when she was very young and had my sister to protect her from me. My sister believed in tough love. I had no intentions on staying that long, anyway. I spent three months in Georgia Regional after explaining it was KKK night when I was detained. The Clayton County psychiatrist agreed. "It probably was," she said, when I was apprehended. I fasted for thirty-nine days.

My card-game buddies were said to have been murderers who were contending with the judicial system. A Moslem male I had befriended was affiliated, he said, with Brother Rap Brown, a black activist who was vying with his own judicial issues. My friend wanted Brother Brown to pull some strings for exoneration. While imprisoned, I lost full circulation of blood in my legs and could not walk. The only known remedy was support hose with elevation to relieve the swelling. I remember the county doctor was white as paper and clearly exhibited his displeasure in diagnosing my condition. They first thought it was Lou Gehrig's disease, but slowly, I regained the activity of my limbs.

I was incarcerated at the time of 9/11, and saw everything as it unfolded on CNN. That fateful day, I was in Georgia Regional Hospital, where I led prayer for staff because we all had concerns. I believed the Feds would blame their enemy, so I volunteered to pray for the truth without one-sidedness by the people. They say there are two sides to a story and the truth. Osama Bin Laden and his people continued to die as martyrs for their country. It was something I was not willing to do.

Around the 9/11 date, Satan and his demons (evil spirits) were in heavy warfare with the Holy Ghost (Holy Spirit) and I. Jesus chose not to have done it on His own. We needed a small army and help from Osama because of his military know-how to annihilate the adversary. I believed the FBI and Army affiliates have this world so deceived by its red, white, and blue colors that they continued to take my power for granted and jeopardized the system with the usage of weapons of mass obstruction—the black arts.

America has not stopped to acknowledge their part in the profound loss of blood it has contributed to the act of war over the years. Jesus's actions and support of the dream giver who marked a term of life only trustworthy noblemen and astute people could adhere to his plan of peace. His breastplate of righteousness in the world superseded the injustices of the United States.

God gave Osama a plan in a vision, like the dream by Dr. King, to defend his people and his country. The holy war I fought with the Word of God by the power and faith vested in me rewards the wisdom of his victorious conquest in the twenty-first century. Jesus gave dreams and visions to His people. I thought Osama must have known Jesus was a little more than just a prophet. His vision really impregnated the height of terrorism in our "free world." Take heed, and note the economic downward spiral into another Great Recession in a century of more. Take heed, and note the fear of wars and plagues where the delineation of overcoming is gray and not a sign of sure victory.

Osama Bin Laden plotted the attack a year before because he had a vision, and revealed his plans, as documented by ABC. Jesus allowed the war to be on American soil because I too needed a small army, which has grown in leaps and bounds since weapons of mass destruction were not found in Iraq. Saddam would show the United States that he had his big guns pointed at them and he was not afraid. Jesus allowed the attack on American soil and approved mainly by my voice after twenty years of suffering in terrorism for Rev. Dr. King, my Lord and God Almighty.

I believed that with what the FBI put me through, America should have gone bankrupt. He knew the ending at the beginning. A holy war was the easiest decision I ever made in my entire life but not only the deadliest. In the salvation process, I reviewed questions in the time of victory and His plan of faith. I wanted the Feds to stop troubling me. I seldom asked questions of God during the assault. Repentance, sanctification, deliverance or recovery, healing, and spirituality were significant in God's care of me. Osama, like Dr. King, wanted to live a long life, but for a cause priced for freedom so costly that their demise prophesized awe. Their mission for their people was magnanimous as winners with purpose and tribute.

On 9/11, I had mixed emotions, because the attack on me was still very heavy. This was the country of my birthplace. I knew a firefighter. I grew up with Vernon Cherry, who sacrificed his life for his beliefs and fellowmen. I thought they all did. Only when I saw that Osama had a white-man issue did I learn and understand his mission for his people. He treated them as if they were born to die for their religious beliefs. Nevertheless, I felt their lives were worthy and justified to live like anyone else. Jesus knew I was heavy under assault by my own government who was just as ruthless, dangerous, and merciless. I wanted to live and raise my child. Attacking a child of God, on the other hand, cursed and confronted an archangel like Dr. King was self-destructive and defeating. Their demonic force spiritually revived principalities, powers of this world and afflicted this heavenly-bound saint of God after twenty years of absolute punishment by physical suffering. Jesus needed to impart wisdom to a visionary to use as vessels, like Osama.

Osama and his men introduced this nation to suicide by planes. In my opinion, they were just as competent as the UN Security Council. I wanted the UN to assist when I was writing to them about my problem. All they needed to do was question the air traffic controller because I gave them a date and a time. I thought my adversaries frequented the New York tristate area thereafter often. I believed Osama urged to wage war against the Feds by Jesus's righteousness of war and His consecration of me deemed necessary. I stood for my rights as well by the nature of His laws on vengeance.

The Almighty God, with omnipotence overriding systematic tactics and woes of punishment, victoriously remained on the world stage of His government and the elect by fulfilling the law sought for a people saved by grace. I believed it was a war the FBI waged against an omnipotent, omniscient and omnipresent God, my Savior. I closed all my letters, "In Jesus's name and He as my witness."

Justice combined over thirty-one years of my life of a long, arduous, and compelling battle to overcome a life of psychiatric malpractice by a pharmaceutical range of pills. Pills enhance the chemistry and precipitate their mind-altering side effects it was made to subside, like paranoia. Their drugs decanoate shots of life controlled by state law as being an accomplice of human error, which threatened the change in my belief system. I can become delusional without the meds and paranoid for the very illness it is trying to treat. I haven't been paranoid since the eighties, when I stopped looking over my shoulder. I paid the price and did my own testing by noncompliance of the medication.

Osama recognized a gall, cunning subtlety of the white man he dared to differ with and had a vision. The strong arm I saw in a dream was punitive toward a people who have their own self-interests. He chose the right to exercise liberty in his country, an act that was met with aggravation by his family and resistance from the Saudi Arabia regime (ABC). The privacy to conduct business as he saw fit developed into a rage and hard life for us all. The privacy to conduct business and free other lands does not need the policing and retaliation by the United States all the time. Introspection of approval by this world power is not always acceptable to other countries. ReRection of suicide is the key to sustain the masses of Osama's peep into the future for his army. Protection by the most elaborate plans fuels and infiltrates the power source with his transparency of terrorism. Osama documented his plans of belief (ABC).

Suicides of peace for me aid this black American in my sanctuary of humility, coming with a price that was costly and effective. I thought the president unknowingly became a trailblazer of the rights of others through studies of country Western lifestyles to collaborate the time through unchartered waters of trouble to attack the just as unfair. I believed the Obama administration backed the franchise of failures and lives of the white man who could never kill the spirit and soul of our leaders.

Osama was highly respected by many in his native land of Moslem persuasion. This full-Redged war inoculated his people with a mission, which can never regain the strength of God to seize tranquil waters of peace ever again—not like this.

My last institutionalization at Elmhurst Hospital, I waited for several months for an SRO in a community-living program in Brooklyn. It is a program for people with a diagnosis. I was homeless. Had anyone asked me about ever wanting to reside in Brooklyn, my answer would still be a resounding no. I perceived Brooklyn to be too remote from Queens. I could never pay the rent on a case manager's salary nevertheless on a Social Security disability check anywhere alone. This is a Jewish organization, and I gratefully took lodging for the mentally challenged.

I continued to follow my worship at a local Baptist Church. I complained about the organization exercising Judaism strictly but I do not get the same respect. I have to fast and pray. I believed in Jesus to solve this spiritual problem totally, which should be acknowledged with respect. That's my faith.

That's my religion.

I joined the church and attended Sunday school, Bible study besides Sunday-morning worship, anniversaries, and special programs for better days. I moved to Crown Heights a year later but continued to tithe and give an offering faithfully. I disclosed to Pastor the King occurrence and why I used to live in the residence on the corner. He taped our private conversation without my consent. He also had a deacon sit in for sexual harassment protection, they say. I was furious when Pastor allowed a visiting church to play the battle hymn of the Republic before service. Did he not realize that the American Rag was God's enemy too, or did he not keep my business to himself? Let me mention that the deacon was a good friend of mine. I thought it was inappropriate, and walked out. Where else am I to get refuge other than church from this mean world?

I moved to the Crown Heights area and started working for Little Flower Children Services as the housing specialist. Intermittently, I took the medication prescribed. I suffered the consequences at mental health court, with the help of my family. I changed my Baptist discipleship to where the shepherd of the house indirectly had ties to Dr. King. I presented my plight to him on paper.

After four years, Pastor rejected me and had three representatives visit in Woodhull Hospital. Pastor would tell anyone he does not do hospitals, and he didn't. I paid my tithes, personal gifts, and offerings, so he had to send someone.

"What you want me to do?" he asked. "Pray for me," I told him.

He did not befriend or acknowledge anyone "unless they had their master's degree." He said, anyway. I guess I was too personal or too friendly for him.

Sister Mary from Augusta always told me to leave that church in Brooklyn regardless of how close I could be to the memoirs and legacy of Dr. King. I shared my vision with him. But he snubbed me for the last time one Sunday during service. He was arrogant and self-righteous. I brought a lot of my Christian experience by the Word of God to the table. But I still was the class clown. He left a lot to be desired as a graduate with a master's degree in theology or divinity. He did give me a reference to Kings County Medical Center for their peer counselor program for employment. The last pastor said about that to his surprise, "You mean you got that job?" I failed to perceive anything wrong with it. It was a job in the middle of a recession, and one that I enjoyed.

I started working for Kings County on September 13, 2010. This satellite program as a peer counselor welcomed persons who had a diagnosis into the mental health field. As a mental health aide, I related to a "recipient of care," as so noted by Dr. Miriam Azaunce instead of patient or client. Mental health today is more successful because we are treated as more humane by gentler terms, such as someone with a diagnosis rather than being termed "insane," "loco," "crazy," or "bugged out." I could assist in advocating for the consumer with the professional teams, which consisted of a psychiatrist, psychologist, social worker, and community liaison. I represented the community and shared some of my experiences having a diagnosis.

As peer counselor, the intensity of quality of care by my expertise assisted in aiding the client back into the community and ultimately back into mainstream society by employment. This is what I wanted for the recipients rather than a check every month. But they had to want it for themselves. I found most of them to be basically unmotivated, and a disability check was all they wanted out of life. They needed a higher-education plan. Those who were overcoming the illness had no skills or a trade. The mental health field has advanced and made great strides of care in this satellite program. Kings County has the largest in the nation.

Woodhull Mental Health Hospital of Brooklyn remains in 2015 to be the worst hospital I have been institutionalized in. It has unsanitary conditions, and patients can be coded for this neglect. I demanded better conditions and was coded for not following orders. Staff lied to cover up their incompetency at my expense. Woodhull had bugs and a vermin infestation. It lacked a reliable maintenance crew. Unfortunately, I had an 18-carat gold bracelet my sister brought me from Italy, which was never documented upon admittance. Personnel stole it because I forgot I carried it with me for repair in my pocketbook. I always wanted that to be the last hospitalization. The program had me committed even though I had no symptoms for noncompliance for three months. Deliverance does not prevail in this Jewish organization or in mainstream society. My God is better than that. It is His Word at stake here.

I got a court date to plead my case, but the legal instrument was not delivered to me on time. After six to eight weeks of being noncompliant, the chief of staff, my doctor petitioned the courts. Experience fell on behalf of the system. So I took the meds that Monday although Thursday was my court date. After being locked up, I began to act out after a month had lapsed like I belonged there. I was livid. They had nothing on me except my residential program insisted upon hospitalization.

I resigned from Kings County in February of 2015. My God looked at me as an African queen. Also, I refuse to tell other peers to take their medication when I don't believe a daily dose is necessary. This is the beauty of taking the medication. You feel better, but gradually, you begin to decompensate. I did not learn to take mine but was forced under the program and NY State law to comply. I realized later that this was a case for the Union. I had no longer a support system in the Hospital Administration.

I believed Kings County was out of line in their questioning me because of a totally different matter regarding my immediate supervisor. The first question they asked me was whether I was taking my meds. It had turned out they were trying to build a case against me for questions about procedures and policy. With a diagnosis, it has got to be my fault. I felt like I was a criminal in my workplace as I was escorted off the premises. The administrator told me to go home for a couple of days. He did not know my job was to counsel the recipient of care and consult. I told him that it was my job, and the supervisor said nothing. She was the one with amnesia. My residence was at stake, but he insisted that I go. I knew then I was resigning.

A three-year relationship with a bitter, mean, cruel, obese, bipolar Southern white Baptist cussed me out about talking to her concerning God. She was a threat despite the recipient of care telling them we sometimes talk about religion as well as politics. I was doing my job, and she was not on my caseload but was a patient, nevertheless. I was doing a former social worker on my caseload a favor by listening to her patient's problems practically every day. Even she said nothing to her boss. She was too busy. My supervisor interrogated me with legal papers. Two days later, in front of her supervisor, she said she forgot, like she had a diagnosis. Jesus is a part of me now in lifestyle, and I am proud to be a disciple. He has done too much for me to deny Him.

Their promotion procedures were questionable also. Because of my hospitalization, I missed out. My coworker, who was a freshman in college and a business major, got the five-thousand-dollar raise as case manager- community liaison. She had some caseworker experience but was never called in for a second interview when I was there. I really should have gotten the promotion because I was worthy. As a result, the hiring manager had to call me in for a second interview for the Outpatient Department position for procedure purposes. She interviewed me with her mind made up on another candidate. As a matter of formality, we went through the motions since the beginning of August 2014. I hope Kings County didn't think I was going to work in the same outpatient office as a peer counselor. I would have resigned first.

This lifetime sentence will forever keep me at odds with the system. People still have to be educated about life with a diagnosis. We cannot stand alone in the truth. The patient or recipient of care will lose every time in contrast to someone without a diagnosis. At Woodhull, the chief of psychiatry had not a clue about Christianity, and was a homosexual. So who was I going to talk to about what discomforts I had with staff and mental health life? Homosexuality is an abomination to my God. I thought he had a psych problem he was dealing with. We still love them, but I don't want to listen to anyone but the preacher regarding my unholy mind problem when you have one.

Woodhull did not understand about fasting, faith, praying without ceasing, and hearing the Word of God. It was absurd. Dare I discuss powers of the rulers, witchcraft, or Harry Potter sorcery matters to anyone? The hospital had many policies for patient rights but did not adhere to them. The so-called professionals will lie like I'm stupid. No one explains to you about patient rights as a recipient of care. They did not abide by them, regardless. There we have ample time to listen about our rights and would be a good group lesson.

Gracie Square is where I learned about the seventy-two-hour hold if one voluntarily commits themselves. As much as I am against hospitalization when it comes to me, I was concerned about my seventeen-year-old, and committed myself. I wanted to stress the importance of her actions in life and how her mistakes affect me. I wrote a letter and was released in three days. That is all hospitalization was ever necessary in my case. My attitude is, "Just give me the meds so I can leave," and that is all they can do for me.

IN THE SPIRIT OF JESUS CHRIST

I called on Jesus to wipe away my years of mental anguish. I called on Jesus to heal the brokenhearted. I called on Jesus to heal the wounds of life and the bitterness my country has grieved me to forgive. I questioned Jesus repeatedly. "How do you forgive Satan?" In my opinion, my country has taught me who they are by their very supernatural subterfuge, which solemnly tipped the scales to Satan. If it were not for Jesus, I would have been dead decades ago. If it were not for Jesus, I would have left Creedmoor as a broken woman instead of working in a hospital as a peer counselor. Jesus, by whose very name demons tremble and Satan has to Bee.

Jesus showed Himself to me as a mighty judge through Osama as a God of vengeance, wrath, and justice. In my opinion, the United States lives in the aftermath of paid repercussions and consequences for sin. I believed the unrepentant heart of a nation condescends destiny to lose a battle with a child of God as joint heirs with Christ (Gal. 3:29) of the kingdom of the Father who we call "Abba," Jehovah, God (Rom. 8:15). God cannot lie (Num. 23:19). Overall, I thank Him for His peace of mind and spiritual rest.

Justice for me as a child of the King reigns and rules prevalent in my mind (John 16:33) as an overcomer. The Spirit of the living God settled fair and square as I grace each day with the will to live with a brand-new mercy. I am amazed and astonished by the solitude of a one-woman army that prevailed in this war of insanities, injustices, and outpouring of a supernatural negative force against omnipotence.

I thought the FBI by command of criminal assault personnel perpetrated lawlessness throughout this season of strife and wrath as a lone Army military might. I believed their determination and urge to kill the soul, body, and spirit transcend into Jesus's love for His bride (church) and His body or members. His sovereignty remained, reigned, and supported my victory by His power unmatched despite the occult.

I believed reverse psychology stemmed from the aptitude of a demented mind as a predator who feared his own serpent's shadow, which instinctively made him angrier. His frightening character was indicative of a worse-than- ever display of a fool's rage at its Creator for divulging this large sum of money. Satan's mission was unbelievably a hardening of the heart as accomplices who embraced this feud for the curdling of their blood for me. I believed money matters were already discussed with Dr. King as the deranged man saw fit to direct my mind and soul with his terrorism as works of negativity full of dark powers. As a woman with a spiritual eye and ear who focused on Christ's leadership and justice, God rebuked the posttraumatic stress disorder of battle fatigue by these variant styles of spirits upon the human mind and the human head. Overall, Satan does not have all power.

This schizophrenia chemical disorder according to scientists was irrational, delusional and an admittance of being in denial on my part (if that is your claim) to the end of this savagery for His people. I will never concede to the schizophrenia in my life that was forced upon me. But now that which lingers in the spirit is due to the meds. My mind inevitably ceased the ungodly war game of attacks to the body. Words of love terminated the enemy from seeping their forbidden blood into my arteries with gall. Saddam Hussein, Osama Bin Laden, and Al Qaeda operatives spurn the development of intense planning by the craft of combat that counterattacks them. I admire these men of valor for exercising their rights against superpowers as the United States who extensively punished me for my hearsay rights as a citizen and invaded my privacy (Acts 4:20). This subjects America to nuclear war as atomic warheads and rumors of the use of uranium in post-9/11 combat on American soil increase by Kim Jong Un and Iran.

I believed the Feds assert themselves as being pompous, self-righteous, law-enforcing, strong-armed, and brave tactical men who blame the inside work of suicide cartels for their festering hatred of America. My season of blessings subjected me to ingenuity of defense by a holy war despite the odds and efforts by the adversary to deny their loss. In March 2009, I declared to be more than a conqueror due to a recession and global terrorist acts as their spirits lapse into another year.

In my opinion, the Federal Bureau of Investigation forewarned of their right to perform unclean, merciless, and foolish wickedness as terrorists. The next course of action increased their magnitude against Jesus in a strategic stance for them to be successful as combatants of ill repute by war waged, as He laughs. I am overwhelmed with a victorious spirit as a God-given source of strength and sovereignty in the kingdom of the King of kings and Lord of lords. I presume this holy war for justice, peace, freedom, and equality and these records of accountability that are well hidden by now under said sexual ploys of profanity have disintegrated covers that have returned to the pit of hell. Vengeance is mine. I shall repay says the Lord (Rom 12:19). As a believer and a witness, I am satisfied with His actions. I stand in awe of these evil and last days because this is their war—the war of the Antichrist, the war of the False Prophet (1 Cor. 15:12-19).

Jesus speaks clearly and audibly in "a small still voice" (Kings 19:12) while the offending evil spirits put you on blast about their position. Jesus has never talked to me in His way but streams His message to me. My Besh streams too. I have asked for a spirit of discernment to make sure there is no mistake about Him. Satan, or the Antichrist in the spirit realm, never closes his mouth and is always on cue. This is by design. You would be amazed to hear them clearly defend the words of cross nitwits sometimes inside my head.

I believed these animals have more intelligence in the spirit realm than in this world. I counteracted with words from the Bible and pleaded lately the Blood of Jesus was against them. Praise and worship are other spiritual weapons I used in battle. In addition, now His glory would see me through hard times.

My situation relieved me to adhere to the written word of judgment from a judicial and civil rights position from my spirit and soul. It was the evil deeds by demons that could impact their wicked affect and effect on my life. My delusional thoughts stem from their constant barbaric statements and actions of knowing Christ's power but are until recently rarely harmful or violent in my behavior. I argued about this. I am not a violent person. My Besh wanted me to hit the nurse so I could go home. Apprehensively, I jabbed at her, and she ran out the room. That was the end of that.

I marveled at the wonderful works of Jesus by the Holy Spirit to commit justifiably His will. I was exposed to graciously accept his miracles as a God at war. This intrigue heightened my faith as my worship intensified. I became a radical for Christ, a feeling that burned deep in my soul. The loving relationship predisposed me to love my God and shine His glory in my lifestyle.

Jesus and the Father told me how precious I was as a lady. I don't mind being the apple of their eyes or the African queen of my house. He can express His sweet love for me at any time. I am happy about the way they romance me. The will to keep running the race for thirty-more years was all right with me. Consequently, I will make mention of hindsight if I could only have said no to myself, something Bishop Noel Jones pointed out at the age of sixteen. Regrettably, I must admit it would have changed the course of my life because I knew better since the Railroad decades ago.

In contrast, I perceived the FBI subjected and forced their employment on me while I had no choice but to withstand their merciless spirits for a loathsome cause of satanic wiles to kill. Death spiritually consumed their life to subject my privacy to outside sexual pressure from their lord and his wicked mind to hate. Sometimes, I thought it is fair to note their lack of fear of God by the aggressor pointed fervently toward their own death. By their own confession, they were sorry too.

I waited patiently to perceive the accuracy of their work release by the Word of Christ as the Son of God and Calvary believer to Bee. The Spirit of Jesus induced and provoked by a holy war of economic proportions and the fright- night Bight for the honor of Dr. King to the federal wizardry of gall and attempted murder on my person came to lessons learned by all. I believed the normlessness and lawlessness experience has taught me to attest that the admitted sociopath and racist followers are alive and well in high places since the Reagan administration. I thought it was an era of concealing and destroying evidence of accountability by evil spirits as the truth in terms of divine intervention went forth.

As fearful powers of darkness, Jesus repeatedly kept me safe in his arms and on guard as I endured to the end a massacre of forbidden glory of silence. Jesus adjured me to stay the course and live a life wholesome to my calling. The honesty for the saint of God developed into mayhem. The mind of fear factors affected me in my total being. Moreover, I was afraid of what clearly was abnormal constructs of their mind due to the supernatural.

The hostility of electrifying waves of fearfulness circumvented the physical body. The attempt to assault and murder kept my overcoming life of worship, praise, and fasting during spiritual warfare basically through prayer. I realized they could not kill me after years of trying, and obviously, I was not suicidal. I thought it was unfair for me to feel that way.

Satan sought daily the divine nature of the living God which indwells as I suffered in learning the true enchantment of negative energies of sorceries (Isa. 47:12-13). An omnipotent positive force—the Holy Spirit—inspired my life by correcting the seeming standstill cry of the sick, with a lifestyle of curses, illicit drugs, profanity, and sex. His mercy endures forever (Ps. 136:1) while the grace of God permeated my left hemisphere. He anointed my head with oil and healed the sick while blessings rid their creation of compelling acts by their laborious Burry of mental cruelty and unrest.

Jesus harvested the attacks for my correction as a combatant for Christianity, a warrior for Christ. I was saved by the clutches of His righteousness because He loves me. The sanity I kept and the sanctity of it led to persecution embodiment of immorality by the opposing god. Jesus loved me with an everlasting love. My heart supernaturally acquired the agape love (unconditional) by the outreach of His most precious blood as other identifiers angered and fueled the attacks.

By another god at work, which was preposterous and preponderance, Satan meant it for evil. But God meant it for my good (Rom. 12:21). As a result, Jesus Christ the Anointed One served as the Master and Orchestrator who came to my delight. My sorry state of affairs that strengthened my heart to feel the love, peace, forgiveness, and gratitude abided gracefully. Above all, the cowardice attempts to silence my heart grew in the promise of deliverance and recovery. Trevor was gone. Jesus honored me with His undying, unfailing, never-ending love of a father figure throughout this ungodly period. I thought He even cried for me and did on occasion think of no other way to relieve me of my misery. He allowed this holy war.

I believed my unrest and technical support into a paranoia contest by the oppressor continued the abuse of my body until it ceased and resumed to the head. I thought they tried to confuse me with a mind in dark places of havoc.

The pain subsided as the Holy One worked beyond the grave as a small army of white shirts, with military might on a chauvinistic watch with women ultimately protecting the sham, pressed onward. The Holy Spirit journeyed in a conquest of mostly horrific silent nights, which slated intervention with His voice in review. King Jesus elated me. Finally, I realized "it is finished" (John 19:30). My God has acknowledged the codes outside of an institutional setting in the spiritual sphere. God honored the restoration of His piety, peace, love, and joy spiritually to diminish the plot in the background.

The Great Intercessor, Jesus the Christ, encouraged me to pray my way through the dark nights of battle that ensued. He comprehended the moans and the groans. Translation by the Holy Spirit into a sense of going through two heavens by way of frantic SOS appeals and sponsorship of great wisdom was faith filled days due to His death at Calvary. Often, I had to battle alone.

Despite the discomfit, I trusted Him to make me see this victory like none other in US history by this modern-day version of war in the supernatural. The Antichrist could never slay that which is eternally good. The concealing of facts that cripple a nation share undisclosed evil tactics that curtail my right to live freely and peacefully. Revenge due to opposing sides of color in mankind was ruthless and despicable to the Creator.

I believed a Supreme Being called me amid the hostility and an attack on the light of Dr. King as characters from law enforcement vessels dominating in the spiritual realm of this world reigned temporarily. The violent streak of lawlessness to silence me into a state of fear because of Dr. King, by rehashing old wounds from an apathetic demonic force, was however, an immediate loss.

The Spirit of Christ yearned to control as my beacon of hope to secure my rendition of faith and charity but, most of all, His power of love—the Holy Spirit. They could not die a second time. Satan seized the years into a state of gall by self-righteousness as my God promised me to live again in a so-called free country. The confines of the truth maximize absolute power as a steward of opportunities across a spectrum of preventable spiritual broken laws.

In my opinion, the white man had chosen to implement poor judgment and insight by choosing this spiritual war to destroy His principles of Christian living and thinking. The normlessness (anomie) of this outfit penetrated cowardice plots to avenge the Almighty God who dispelled the asunder of marriage. I deduced the USA was under judgment by Jesus due to this horrific pledge of careless and profane work. Terrorism and the economy are by- products of His judgment, and revenge was from the Spirit of the Living God.

For twenty years of torture, my rebelliousness in the mind as a victor has altered the plans for my life. In the twilight and in a twinkling of an eye, justice and now, thirty years later, manipulate the mind to make peace with my God and accept single parenthood stripped of guilt. My servitude of Him and to those with a diagnosis compelled me into the brotherhood of the people without self-pity but with concern. I stopped sleeping around since 2000.

I am a God-fearing woman incumbent against the mistaken loyalty of demonic subterfuge as a sinful soul of schizophrenia. The devil is a liar. With the power based upon my spirituality to stomp on the Devil's neck like treading upon "serpents and scorpions" (Luke 10:19) has up lifted my way. When I was seven years old, my Besh decided as an earthly vessel to live sanctified as one of joy, peace, love, holiness and "acceptable unto God" (Rom. 12:1) to be used to keep from falling into the darkness of cruel missions and sin.

That is now my preventable quest and my purpose. Accusations, assumptions, distractions, deceptions, and devilish antics to test the child of God are insane at fifty-seven as a blood-washed seasoned saint. I had strayed away from my upbringing over fifty years ago and grieved the Holy Spirit. Today, I have learned my lessons well and work with Him. To God be the glory.

DELIVERANCE TODAY: "PEACE BE STILL" (MARK 4:39)

*M*y Christian faith does not fall short of consequences by remorse as a believer. I believed I was haunted by known Fed racist killers, Army veterans and/or sellouts make you wonder how I got over in a dying world of the KKK, sex, profanity, and the black arts. I am just glad to be alive and, therefore, am indebted to my God because I don't have to be a dead, crazy black militant saint. I believed they conspired to haunt as ongoing historical powers of witchcraft and sorcery by African craft of curses in the supernatural. Calling on a prayer warrior to defend is atypical in this day and age. To remind me of His past in an empty borrowed tomb could better awaken the Spirit of holiness of Jesus Christ, and because of His resurrection of His majesty, I live as a forgiven conqueror. I am a part of His royal priesthood as King of the Jews and a prayer warrior.

Mystic fans would offer condolences for those petrified by a grueling team of experts in the black arts against His justification and why He has reshaped this country in global warming. In my opinion, my conquest urges the burning of a law enforcement leader subsequent to this eerie likeminded frenzy of Anabel. Their commitment to this awesome lapse of judgment is horrific. I welcome anticipation of acts warming the heart as my Warrior, by His divine deliverance and soothing style of intervention,

I have come now into a place of grace whereas being a child of God Almighty committed to a divine and acceptable season as worthy of His blessings.

Since I guilt trip and don't have to condemn myself or feel unworthy, I am free. There is therefore now no condemnation to them which are in Christ Jesus (Rom. 8:1). The black arts are almost dead. The reason why there is so much godly unrest and man on the brink of war was due to the lack of accepting Jesus Christ as Savior of the world and an effective prayer life. There should only be a holy war when prayers are answered by the Godhead of Jesus Christ. This is the only way to win a holy war. The Holy Trinity has His function. Grace alone is not enough in the twenty-first century. You have to go through something in order to know Him.

One must come through the Messiah to contact the Father. There is a procedure, and He has a process. To speak to the Father, you must use His protocol. You must come through His Son, Jesus Christ, the Intercessor, about everything and anything in decency and in order. You do not have to commit suicide to win the war now. They paid the price as martyrs. However, there will always be casualties in war. Mine were 9/11. Like the pilots, they probably did not mind dying for their country and beliefs. I told Jesus in 2001. However, the one and only religious sacrificial death was given by Jesus, and no one else can compare to it. So religious suicide today is a sin, because Jesus already paid the price! To God be the glory, and amen!

I stood like Dr. King to live eternally in the Savior's arms. We are to come to Him just as we are as children through Jesus and in His name. He is no respecter of person. You must be born again. With the second spiritual birth, He is willing to perform miracles on your behalf. One does not have to die to win a war with the United States of America, or in any other country. He will give you strength and protect as I write my account.

Salvation is free to all who believe in the death, burial, and resurrection of Jesus Christ. If you believe there was a Jesus Christ, you should actually believe He was more than a prophet or someone omitted this important fact for undermining reasons two thousand years ago (Matt. 28:13). He takes care of his disciples and gives power to His people. He is a forgiving God. I am a living witness of his love and tender mercies. As the Son of Man and as Son of the Father, He opens the door to ask what you will, what you want in life, and until death, he provides. He only asked in return for reverence, love, and obedience.

This world is temporary, and we are only passing through. There will be ups and downs, but "be of good cheer." He has "overcome the world" (John 16:33). He promises you eternal life. Either He can solve anything and everything, or it just cannot be done. Jesus Christ experienced it two thousand years ago, when our Father prepared Him a human body, and we all should know about Christmas or the birth of Christ.

Jesus is a good God, and His grace is sufficient to sustain me in terrorism. "For all have sinned, and come short of the glory of God" (Rom. 3:23) except Christ. He was able to abolish the "law" by fulfilling it.

Since He died on Calvary's cruel cross for the remission of sin, He only asks for you to be sorry or to repent. He knew no sin but became sin for us. So He can pardon all our transgressions and iniquities. After repentance, our Father only sees His Son's blood. There is no more guilt and shame about anything in your past, present, or future. There is no greater love like the grace of God. "No man cometh unto the Father, but by me," Jesus said (John 14:6).

Upon acceptance, Jesus immediately indwells within your heart by the Holy Spirit. Your body houses the Holy Spirit, or the third person of the Godhead or Holy Trinity. Consequently, you are adopted as part of His royal family. For the most part, I am delivered and set free from schizophrenia because I have now a devout Christian lifestyle and I know the Word of God. I say "For the most part" because their spiritual aftermath lingers on in my mind. But this too shall pass. I have faith in God, for spiritual rest and justice are in His hands.

AUTOBIOGRAPHY AND INTRODUCTION OF KIM L. SMALLS

K im L. Smalls was born and raised in the New York City area. The second child born to Mr. and Mrs. Robert Smalls Sr., she attended Ebenezer Baptist Church until she was eighteen. Her father died when she was twelve. She graduated with honors from New Yok Institute of Technology. At twenty, she gave birth to her daughter, who later was raised by her late grandmother Dutch, as she was affectionately known as by her family and friends.

Kim admits she was quite rebellious in her life, indulging in drug usage, cigarettes, and promiscuity. At Kim's first job as a railroad police officer, she was forced out by their Special Investigation Unit and took part in her first miracle on the railroad tracks. There, she was exposed to the KKK.

Kim is African American.

Kim went on to other employment as a case manager for the city and private sectors of business. She was diagnosed with paranoid schizophrenia in 1984 but with great difficulty to live in a "free country" amid racists and killers, whom she believed to be members of the Federal Bureau of Investigation. After she left the railroad in 1981, Kim thought she was followed to her home due to her supernatural power demonstrated on the tracks. In 1983, her privacy was invaded. God saw fit to allow and wake up her deceased father and Reverend Dr. Martin Luther King Jr. for confirmation, love, salvation, correction, and protection.

She believed from 1981 until the year 2015 the KKK and the FBI, with an Army background, desired her demise after intense fighting and struggle in the spiritual realm. Spiritual warfare, according to the King James Version of the Holy Bible, refers to the mentally ill, or a person with a diagnosis. Since 2001, Kim lives with the aftermath of terrorism and torture by their presence, which is still heartfelt, due to the use of powers of darkness and ramifications of other evil spirits. She was given a lifetime diagnosis because of money.

For we wrestle not against flesh and blood, but against principalities, against powers, against the rulers of the darkness of this world, against wickedness in high places (Eph. 6:12). Jesus Christ has judged this country, affecting their money and as a power of this world of terrorism. No weapon formed against me shall prosper and every tongue that rises up against me in judgment shall be condemned (Isa. 54:17). Kim is a one-woman Army who does not have to die because they declare war on behalf of the United States of America. Kim is a winner and a Federal Bureau of Investigation distraction. Will the real King assassin please stand up from insanity to sanity?